I0560213

Praise for *Teaching with Dignity*

"Exactly what is needed now. By focusing on supporting students and teachers to thrive by prioritizing dignity in classrooms and schools, the authors give us reasons to stay hopeful during challenging times."

—**Prof. Christian van Nieuwerburgh, PhD, Professor of Coaching and Positive Psychology, RCSI University of Medicine and Health Sciences, Ireland**

"Learning is ultimately about growing, and this book masterfully cultivates that idea. Using a brilliant agricultural metaphor, the authors illuminate how nurturing a culture of dignity is not about ignoring inequities but about planting the conditions for true educational justice. Like skilled gardeners, educators can disrupt deficit-based narratives and foster an environment where every student, teacher, and administrator flourishes. With compelling case studies, practical tools, and the inspiring story of Summer Snyder, this book offers both the philosophy and the practice to make dignity the fertile ground from which all learning grows. It is a must-read for anyone committed to cultivating meaningful change in education."

—**Michelle A. Bowman, EdD, Senior Vice President, Networks & Continuous Improvement, Learning Forward**

"Dignity is one of the most important concepts to understand if you want to create the schools our kids deserve. And no one has taught me more than John Krownapple and Floyd Cobb. In this new book, they describe how to weave dignity into every aspect that matters in the classroom: student engagement, instruction, learning environment, and routines and expectations, to name a few."

—**Jim Knight, PhD, Author of *The Definitive Guide to Instructional Coaching***

"I came for the hands-on strategies to honor dignity in classrooms and stayed for the self-deprecating footnotes. Teaching with Dignity takes the somewhat nebulous concept of dignity and explains it in a tangible way through the metaphor of a garden. Add in real-life examples from master teacher Summer Snyder and easy-to-read prose, and I'm sold! EVERY classroom can be a dignity garden with this book. John and Floyd prove that building belonging isn't something extra. It's essential."

—**Kimberly Strong, Director of Teacher and Student Engagement, High Desert Education Service District, Central Oregon**

"Krownapple, Cobb, and Snyder make a powerful case that dignity is the foundation for compassionate and effective teaching. They provide clear but flexible steps for establishing a positive culture where every student and educator is valued and supported by clear expectations and thoughtful responses, all so that each individual can thrive."

—**Kent McIntosh, PhD, Philip H. Knight Chair of Special Education, University of Oregon**

"As a teacher (and a parent) working and raising kids within systems that don't always appear to prioritize dignity, this book was a breath of fresh air. The clear examples of how teaching with dignity can play out in the classroom helped me feel empowered to create environments that nurture the dignity of my students and my own children. The authors reminded me, over and over, that teaching (or parenting) with dignity is not about eliminating challenges but helping capable learners navigate them with independence and integrity."

—**Lindsey Kiersey, MEd, Teacher, Special Education Social Studies, Rockwood School District, Missouri**

"Teaching with Dignity is an inspiring and transformative guide for educators. It's packed with practical strategies and real-life examples that show how to create a classroom where every student feels valued and empowered. It's a must-read for any school administrator passionate about fostering a positive and inclusive school culture!"

—**Dr. Shawn Dutkiewicz, Assistant Superintendent of Teaching and Learning, Radnor Township School District, Pennsylvania**

"To thrive, we all need to feel like we belong. Building and nurturing a culture of dignity is the key to achieving this. John Krownapple and Floyd Cobb guide us to become thoughtful, intentional cultivators of dignity-centered teaching. Along with Summer Snyder's invaluable, real-world examples and practical tools, the authors empower us to transform thoughts and words into meaningful actions."

—**Tim Clarke, Assistant Superintendent for Instructional Services, Cattaraugus-Allegany-Erie-Wyoming BOCES, New York**

"As a DEI practitioner, this is the breath of fresh air we have all been waiting for! Teaching with Dignity moves beyond theory and provides practical guidance on implementing this work in your school community. For busy educators who are consumed by the day-to-day of school life and don't have time for yet "another thing," John, Floyd, and Summer provide ready-to-go examples, based on their own experience, of how to center dignity as the anchor in your school community. Their framework is something that all those who work in schools should strive to adopt to achieve systemic and institutional improvements."

—**Delonte Egwuatu, Chief Engagement & Inclusion Officer, Beaver Country Day School, Massachusetts**

"If you're an exhausted educator searching for a spark, Teaching with Dignity delivers. And let's be honest—any book that quotes Yoda and makes you believe in the power of your work again? That's worth your time."

—Christine Boone, MEd, Assistant Superintendent, District Development, RSU 22, Maine

"Powerful and relatable, this book offers a fresh perspective on the importance of dignity-centered teaching. With contributions from Summer Snyder, the book provides educators with practical strategies for creating a nurturing and inclusive learning environment where all students can thrive. Its thoughtful approach emphasizes emotional and intellectual well-being, encouraging teachers to honor their students as whole individuals. This book is essential for anyone passionate about transforming education by utilizing a framework for learning and growth that honors dignity in the classroom."

—Jill M. Karp, EdD, Deputy Superintendent, Merrick Union Free School District, New York

"As a teacher, I always used the word respect: Respect your elders, respect others in this classroom, respect others' property, etc. However, in my current role, I have seen how shifting to, modeling, and embodying the concept of dignity changes behavior and hearts. In Teaching with Dignity, John, Floyd, and Summer encapsulate the deep understanding that students can understand their inherent value and worth through the right classroom conditions, allowing them to value others simply because we are all human beings. I am excited about how this book will create a new understanding of the treatment of others, but more importantly, the treatment of self."

—LaDonna Gulley, EdD, Director of Leadership and Empowerment, Mesquite Independent School District, Texas

"As the leader of the Southern Oregon Regional Educator Network, I've witnessed John Krownapple and Floyd Cobb's work become a guiding light for transforming schools in my region. And Teaching with Dignity with Summer Snyder is taking their collective vision to new heights. Through a brilliant fusion originally based on Donna Hicks' 10 Elements of Dignity, they offer Jedi-level insight for educators to resist the dark side of fear, deficit thinking, and exclusionary practice. Instead, they elicit courage, compassion, and connection while focusing on solutions and co-creating conditions where more people can feel safe, know they matter, and experience true belonging. This book is more than a resource—it's a call to action for anyone ready to create thriving schools rooted in dignity, inclusion, and hope."

—Heidi Olivadoti, Ed.D., Southern Oregon Regional Educator Network (est. 2019), Southern Oregon Education Service District

Copyright © 2025 John Krownapple, Floyd Cobb, and Summer Snyder

Teaching with Dignity: How to Cultivate Classroom Ecosystems Where People Thrive

All rights reserved.

No part of this publication may be reproduced, distributed, or transmitted in any form or by any means—including photocopying, recording, or other electronic or mechanical methods—without the prior written permission of the publisher, except in the case of brief quotations used in critical reviews or scholarly works.

For permission requests, write to the publisher at:

Dignity Works Press

dignityworkspress.com

teachingwithdignity.com

ISBN: 979-8-9991800-0-1

Book design by Chase Christensen

Edited by Alison Hope

First edition 2025

Teaching with Dignity

How To Cultivate Classroom Ecosystems Where People Thrive

**DIGNITY
WORKS
PRESS**

JOHN KROWNAPPLE AND **FLOYD COBB**

WITH SUMMER SNYDER

Table of Contents

Foreword

When John Krownapple and Floyd Cobb asked me to write the foreword to their new book (written with Summer Snyder), I gladly accepted. Since we are all dedicated to advancing the implementation of dignity education in schools, we have worked together for several years to make that aspiration a reality. Their new book, *Teaching with Dignity*, is a giant step toward that goal.

I am writing this foreword today at a time when many people in the United States are feeling uncertain and anxious about the future of public education and other key institutions. However, when I was reading *Teaching with Dignity*, I felt like I was given a new reason to hope. My mentor, Professor Herbert Kelman, told me that one of our most important jobs as educators and peacemakers is to create space for hope to endure. In this case, the authors have filled that space with invaluable information for teachers to make educating in the classroom with dignity an achievable goal.

Hope was alive in teacher Summer Snyder's second-grade classroom. I was astonished that second graders could grasp the power of dignity. Not only did they grasp it, but, most importantly, they internalized and integrated it into their classroom every day. The authors have created an opportunity for all students in all classrooms, regardless of grade level or cognitive capacity, to start their lives with a blueprint for developing relationships of all kinds on a foundation of dignity.

Not only have the authors developed a clear and understandable road-map for teachers and students to follow in their pursuit of a dignity culture in their lives and classrooms, but they have also given their students the felt experience of dignity. It is far more than an intellectual exercise. Being told that they all have inborn value and worth is one thing. For them to feel that inherent worth is another. The book gives countless examples of how teachers can create that feeling of worth in their students by treating them with dignity.

I have always believed that, along with the ABC's, all students should be exposed to the ABCD's! The D's contribution (dignity) could enhance human connection in a way that could significantly contribute to the well-being and flourishing of all humanity. My vision, and that of the authors, is to create the conditions for all of us to live in peace. As my other mentor, Archbishop Desmond Tutu, reminded me, there is no such thing as democracy without dignity, and there is no peace in the world without the awareness of the inherent worth of all human beings. If we can instill this fundamental truth about humanity in our students as young as second graders, it is altogether possible that if all teachers in all grades were trained in *Teaching with Dignity*, we just might have a chance to shift the way we live together in the world. The shift would embrace our shared humanity and the recognition that all human beings, born with inherent worth, deserve to be treated with dignity.

I have worked with students from all over the world, and one thing that is common to them all is their shared desire to be treated as if they matter. I have come to believe that our shared yearning to be treated with dignity is our highest common denominator. We can all rally around that shared desire, and John Krownapple, Floyd Cobb, and Summer Snyder have paved the way for us to achieve it.

Donna Hicks, PhD

Associate at the Weatherhead Center for International Affairs, Harvard University, and author of *Dignity: Its Essential Role in Resolving Conflict* and *Leading with Dignity: How to Create a Culture That Brings Out the Best in People.*

About the Authors

John Krownapple is an educator passionate about education, learning, and helping people reach their full potential. Whether teaching, writing, speaking, or facilitating professional learning, he helps educators explore the conditions that help people thrive. John began his career as an elementary school  teacher in Howard County, Maryland, in 1996, after earning a degree in Elementary Education from the University of Maryland, College Park. He later earned his master's degree in Administration and Supervision from Loyola College in Maryland. Over the years, he has served as a district-level curriculum specialist, professional development facilitator, and organizational development administrator. Additionally, he was an adjunct professor at The Johns Hopkins University for 17 years. Since 2014, John has partnered with numerous schools and districts as an educational consultant, and in 2020, he cofounded Dignity Consulting LLC.

 Floyd Cobb, PhD, is an accomplished educator with 25 years of leadership across the early childhood through higher education continuum. He has served as a teacher, school leader, district curriculum leader, and statewide policy implementer. As the Associate Commissioner of Student Learning at the Col-

orado Department of Education, Floyd managed the implementation of complex statewide education initiatives, including K–3 literacy, standards revision, special education, student discipline, universal preschool, and English language development. He earned a doctorate in Curriculum and Instruction from the Morgridge College of Education at the University of Denver, where he has been an adjunct faculty member since 2011. Floyd teaches courses on educational policy and social inequality. In 2017, he received the Ruth Murray Underhill Teaching Award for Excellence, which is presented annually to one adjunct faculty member at the university.

Summer Snyder is dedicated to fostering inclusive and equitable classrooms and schools. With more than 20 years of specialized experience in supporting differentiated instruction, she has served as a classroom teacher, instructional coach, and the Differentiation Coordinator for a district that serves more than 55,000 students across eight municipalities in Denver, Colorado. Summer currently works as an independent consultant, leading a range of professional learning and development initiatives focused on helping schools build the capacity to meet diverse needs through inclusive environments where all students and staff feel a sense of belonging because their dignity is honored. Summer's work has earned her multiple accolades, including the Golden Heart Award, the Excellence Award for Organizations, the Superintendent Making a Difference Award, and the 2023 Teacher of the Year for Cherry Creek Schools. She holds bachelor's degrees in Elementary Education and Special Education, and a master's degree in Curriculum and Instruction.

Introduction

Why are so many educators struggling under a system that frustrates their vocation to teach and to help students learn and grow? Are you one of them?

You might feel like the system keeps getting in the way of what you know good teaching requires. Perhaps you feel that your role has been reduced to merely ticking boxes, enforcing regulations, and teaching to the test. Are you bothered that so many teachers, both in the United States and worldwide, are stressed, uninspired, and burned out to the point of quitting? This is true not only in the United States but also in other countries. You're not imagining things. It's real, and it has happened over time. The problem, we believe, is that education has become a marketplace rather than a garden for learning.

Over the past four decades, schooling has adopted values associated with neoliberal educational logic (Starr, 2022). This model applies market-driven concepts to education, focusing on accountability, efficiency, standardization, performance metrics, competition, and control. The broader philosophy prioritizes principles like profit over people and, when applied to education, has stifled the very spirit of teaching. The result? Far too many school environments have become stressful and sterile places where learning is no longer valued for its own sake, and where students are no longer valued as persons. This slow-moving crisis has devolved schooling into a morass of market forces—basically a business.

Are you unfamiliar with neoliberalism? Here are the basics. It's a modern revival of 18th-century free-market capitalism, originally championed by Adam Smith and his concept of the invisible hand. It gathered new steam in the 1970s as a response to economic crises such as stag-flation and the oil crisis, and emphasized a need for limited govern-ment, privatization, competition, and restructuring social programs for market-driven efficiency.

In the 1980s, leaders such as Margaret Thatcher in the United Kingdom and Ronald Reagan in the United States moved neoliberalism from theory to governing doctrine. As neoliberal logic gained traction, its influence extended far beyond markets, reshaping public institutions, such as ed-ucation, to operate under the principles of competition, efficiency, and control. By the late 1980s, Australia had become a global testing ground for outcomes-based education and national standards—strategies that reflect neoliberalism's emphasis on accountability through competition and control.

Historically, though, many societies have regarded education as a public good, one that is essential to developing informed citizens and cohesive communities. Early leaders in the United States, such as Thomas Jeffer-son and John Adams, championed public education as a foundational element of democracy. Across Europe, while educational systems varied widely and were shaped by distinct national histories, most nations and communities established public school systems to advance social welfare and collective well-being. But neoliberalism introduced market-based reforms to education, emphasizing metrics and competition over the common good. This shift has sparked debate over the true purpose of education and who it is ultimately meant to serve.

Some argue that neoliberalism benefits the economy, but we're not here to weigh in on that debate. Our aim is to clearly describe the dominant educational paradigm and offer a strategy for helping people thrive within it (or within any system). After all, the core principles of neoliberalism aren't inherently wrong. Accountability is valuable. It's great, in fact. So is efficiency. But when metrics become the priority, people get lost in the process. The challenge is to keep the focus on people and to ensure that what gets measured never outweighs the people it is meant to serve.

This challenge is significant. The marketplace philosophy now shapes entire systems of schooling—everything from curriculum pacing guides to teacher evaluations and discipline policies. Neoliberalism defines success narrowly, often overlooking the human needs of both students and educators. It easily distorts the innate worth of humans (e.g., their dignity) into a prize to be earned or denied. As such, the system can condition educators to view students as problems to be fixed, rather than as learners to be cultivated. What were once hallowed spaces dedicated to growth and community have become wastelands of control, standardization, and the so-called correction of perceived problems. This is a modern tragedy of epic proportions.

Although neoliberal educational logic normalized the de-centering of dignity in schools, this dehumanizing process most certainly predates the 1980s. For instance, in the United States numerous groups of students (e.g., girls and women, English language learners, students with disabilities, students in poverty, and racial and ethnic minorities) have long navigated educational systems within which they endured demeaning treatment. In other words, for a long time formalized teaching has needed to (and still needs to) cultivate environments that honor dignity by design and default, thereby optimizing the growth and development of all students.

Among many examples, this deficit of dignity-based schooling looks like tacitly or directly steering girls and women away from science, math, and leadership opportunities for most of the 20th century; displacing Black students (and Black teachers) from affirming school communities during desegregation in the 1950s and 1960s; and segregating students with disabilities and treating them as problems. The common thread through any such example is the discriminatory or dehumanizing treatment of students who appeared to be different or deviated from dominant norms.

Schooling in the United States has a long history of distorting or denying human dignity; once you recognize the historical patterns, it's impossible to unsee them. It's fair to say that, while the neoliberal reforms of the 1980s did not invent this dehumanization, they certainly amplified and standardized it. What was once targeted and uneven became institutionalized and accepted. Today, regardless of background, most students and educators operate within systems where compliance and control outweigh connection and care, and where the dignity of both students and educators is often ignored or eroded.

Yet, even as neoliberal logic began to take hold over the past four decades, another mighty force was shaping public education in the United States: the legal legacy of the civil rights era. Over time, landmark legislation—including the Civil Rights Act of 1964, Title IX of the Education Amendments of 1972, the Education for All Handicapped Children Act of 1975 (the Individuals with Disabilities Education Act [IDEA] as of 1990), and Section 504 of the Rehabilitation Act of 1973—extended the protections of the 14th Amendment to public schools. These laws collectively support a legal standard that states all students have a right to be educated with dignity.

Compliance with civil rights law is supposed to set the conditions for dignity within U.S. public schools. Yet, over the decades, persistent educational challenges have proven that legal compliance alone is insufficient.

Implementation matters more. How we interpret, enact, and sustain these legal protections determines whether they truly translate into just, inclusive, and humanizing experiences for students and educators. And the plain truth is that we have not mastered implementation. Academic educators have offered brilliant theories and frameworks for decades, yet effective implementation remains elusive. This is due to an overemphasis on addressing symptoms rather than the root cause. The root cause has always been the lack of dignity built into the educational system. By the term "lack of dignity" we mean systems that fail to recognize all students and educators as whole people, worthy of respect, care, and the opportunity to grow.

That's why we wrote this book: to help cultivate what has been missing all along—an educational culture that prioritizes human dignity above all else.

Incidentally, a dignity-centered approach to education doesn't traffic in slogans like "no excuses" or "take equity by force." These types of mantras may sound bold, but they're usually indistinguishable from the very same systems of control and compliance in desperate need of humane intervention. Emphasizing such slogans risks oversimplifying complex educational challenges and overlooking the importance of compassion within the educational context. Furthermore, a dignity-centered approach doesn't peddle ideas that decouple the work of instruction, learning, and assessment from essential needs such as the need to belong. Thus, teaching with dignity is not about grandstanding, tough talk, machismo, or superficial treatments of trends such as a culture of belonging. Instead, teaching with dignity requires humility and the ability to understand and, when necessary, to transform the conditions that undermine dignity in the first place.

When it comes to teaching with dignity, we discuss theory (of course, we've spent decades studying this subject), but we also guide you through real-life examples of effective implementation. Summer Snyder successfully applied the principles of dignity with her second graders. Don't be fooled into thinking the principles worked because her students were so young! This teaching stance is universal, and it works with our human nature and innate need to have our dignity honored. When dignity is honored, human beings flourish. It's as simple as that, simple enough for second graders. But its simplicity is often difficult for adults to grasp. We hope that, by the time you're finished reading this book, you'll think, "This is so obvious. Why didn't I see it sooner?" So, whether you teach Pre-K, middle school mathematics, a high school biology lab, a community college writing course, or a doctoral seminar, the need to center dignity is urgent.

Yet, dignity remains overlooked, and students continue to be treated as commodities in the marketplace—as products, and not as persons. In early childhood education, play and exploration are often displaced by academic rigor and readiness measures. In secondary schools, discipline systems and performance pressures often crowd out human connection. In higher education, tuition has skyrocketed, access to high-quality institutions has narrowed, and competitive ranking systems have contributed to treating students like customers, professors like content producers, and universities like vendors. Within each level of education, we see how the systems shaped by neoliberal marketplace philosophy have undermined the human essence of teaching: people helping people to grow and learn.

Our book will help you reconnect with this essence, which is the heart of why you chose a career in teaching in the first place.

Let's move on to something in a lighter vein: While the topic of dignity is serious, our footnotes often aren't. That's intentional. You may notice an alarming number of references to pop culture moments from the 1980s. They might seem like inside jokes, and in some ways, they are. But they also reflect our (the authors') terroir—the cultural soil of our upbringing.

Many of our formative years happened during that decade. Although the three of us (John, Floyd, and Summer) grew up in different regions and varying circumstances, that era had a profound impact on us personally and professionally. It was also a turning point in education policy, as the values of neoliberalism began to reshape school systems worldwide. While some of our references are admittedly self-deprecating and nostalgic, they also serve as subtle historical markers of the decade when neoliberal values began shaping education policy around the world. They also highlight the fact that youngsters who appear different (in our case, in terms of race and sex) but who grow up in a common culture will share that cultural connectedness, even when it's not always visible. There really is more that unites us than divides us.

And just as dignity invites connection, so do the cultural moments we share, no matter how ridiculous they are. You might not relate to every reference if you didn't grow up in the 1980s or in the United States. That's okay. We included them anyway because this book is about connection and people. So often human connection starts with something as simple (and maybe as absurd) as the thrill of choosing a new lunch box for the year, of finally getting a coveted Trapper Keeper binder for your school papers, or of recording that song you've been waiting all day for the radio to play so you can finish up your mixtape. Life is good! Enjoy the moments!

A Note on Authorship

John Krownapple and Floyd Cobb wrote this book. We are long-standing thought partners and coauthors, and we speak in a shared voice throughout the text. You'll hear that voice clearly. It reflects years of collaboration, friendship, trust, mutual learning, and countless text messages.

However, this book wouldn't exist without Summer Snyder. Her classroom experience is foundational, and her voice, insight, and leadership are woven throughout the narrative. Far more than a reference or an illustrative example, she is our contributing author. Listing her as an author with us acknowledges both the structure of the writing and the magnitude of her influence.

Together, we offer this book not as a formula, but as a stance. Teaching with dignity is a way of seeing people, navigating systems, and planting seeds for transformation, one interaction at a time.

Welcome. We're thrilled you've chosen to read this book. Let's get to work.

CHAPTER 1

Our Dream: Teaching All Students with Dignity

*Do your little bit of good where you are; it's those little bits
of good together that overwhelm the world.*

—Archbishop Desmond Tutu, 1984

Imagine a Classroom

We have a dream of a better way of teaching. In schools across the world, a growing number of educators are dreaming of something better, too. Prevailing approaches simply aren't working well, not for students, and certainly not for teachers.

Today's world and times have made teaching significantly more diffi-cult than it was even two decades ago, with expanded responsibilities, increased student needs, and shifting expectations (Ingersoll et al., 2014; Kaufman et al., 2024). More on this in a minute, but suffice it to say that too many teachers are struggling under burdens that are too heavy and getting heavier. Too many teachers feel crushed and exhausted. A distressing number have burned out and fled the field.

But it doesn't have to be this way.

We believe that, no matter how bleak things feel, we can dream, imagine, leap, and defy the gravity that's pulling many teachers down into survival mode. Teachers need to thrive, not just survive. So, we're inviting you to join us in building a better alternative. That's what this book is about. The first step toward something better is to imagine something better. Let's take that first step and imagine a better way to teach.

Imagine a classroom where each student feels valued. In this classroom, curiosity, confidence, and belonging fuel learning. Learning is built on connection and engagement rather than compliance. Engagement comes from purpose, not from fear of failure. Teachers see students for their strengths, not their struggles.

Imagine a school and broader community that trusts teachers to focus on what truly matters: inspiring students to learn and building relationships, rather than putting out fires or enforcing ineffective rules. In this school, teaching is about cultivating growth, not just meeting demands or fixing what's broken. Reflection and responsibility are the norm, not fear of shame or punishment.

But for many educators, reality looks far different. The demands of the job have skyrocketed while support has dwindled. Teachers juggle multiple roles: counselors, social workers, and mediators, all while being judged by imposed data points rarely reflecting teachers' true impact on students. Across the world, teachers face a range of similar challenges: student well-being and behavior, cultural expectations, parental pressure, and policy constraints. No matter where you teach, the demands can feel relentless, leaving many wondering how long they can keep going.

The problem isn't teachers. The problem is within educational systems— the complex web of policies, institutional structures, and cultural norms that influence what happens in schools: how students are taught, how teachers are supported or evaluated, and how schools are held account-able. Their typical design prioritizes accountability and compliance over what makes meaningful learning work: connection, trust, and an innate sense of worth for both students and teachers. Without those elements, teaching becomes exhausting, and learning suffers.

The situation is grim, but some educators are turning this boat around. The teachers featured in this book are just a few of the countless educators who are prioritizing and protecting what matters most—the inherent value and worth of people. Their stories offer a solution that works. The way forward isn't simply doing more: it's thinking and working differently, no matter the pressures of your school, district, broader community, or educational system.

That's precisely what Summer Snyder discovered. A veteran educator, former district leader, and now a contributing author alongside John Krownapple and Floyd Cobb, she experienced firsthand how a dehu-manizing system makes educators feel. But she found a way to transform her classroom through the concept of dignity. As a result, Summer was named Teacher of the Year for her Colorado school district.

On the morning that she accepted that award, she wasn't thinking about her success but about every exhausted teacher who shows up for their students every day despite overwhelming challenges. She knew she had to share what she had learned. Because what she discovered wasn't just about what helped her students thrive. It was also about what's possible in every classroom and every school.

Summer's story opens each of our chapters. These real-life scenes offer a blueprint for how to make these ideas—what we're calling teaching with dignity—work in the real world and in ordinary classrooms. Stick with us, and we'll cultivate a path forward. Together.

So, let's begin by meeting Summer.

Summer Snyder's Surprise

The hum of conversation faded as the principal tapped the microphone. A hush settled over the library, full of teachers and other school faculty and staff.

"Dear colleagues, we're setting aside our monthly agenda for something special. One of our own has been named Teacher of the Year!"

Excited murmurs spread through the room. Summer Snyder glanced at a colleague and mouthed, "Who could it be?" Her friend shrugged, eyes widening in curiosity.

Being named Teacher of the Year in a 70-school district was huge, especially after the COVID-19 lockdown, when teaching felt more challenging than ever. The pandemic had disrupted students' academic progress and emotional well-being, and teachers were overwhelmed. Some had even left the profession. But somehow, despite it all, Summer and her students were thriving.

"This year's Teacher of the Year is...Summer Snyder!"

Summer froze. *Did I hear that right?*

The room erupted in applause, and her colleagues rose to their feet. Then she saw her two daughters, both young women now, step onto the stage, carrying balloons and flowers. A lump rose in her throat.

Me? Teacher of the Year? As she walked to the front of the room, memories of the past year rushed in.

This year had been the hardest of her two-decade career. Post-pandemic struggles lingered. She was still grieving the loss of her husband to cancer. This year, she returned to the classroom after working at the district level, a decision she knew was right for her, but not without its challenges.

Though she gained valuable experience, that district-level role had also been brutal. She had seen—no, she had lived—how easily people were reduced to objects: easy to overlook, easy to dismiss. When she produced results, she was celebrated. When she struggled, she was discarded. The system and bureaucracy that claimed to support its educators had dehumanized her, treating her as a data point instead of a human or professional.

At the time, she had no language to explain what had happened. Later, she did. That's when she realized something profound: I haven't been treated with dignity. I don't feel like I really belong here. That experience nearly broke her spirit. It left her questioning everything she once believed about leadership, education, and herself.

Ironically, it also gave her clarity. She had experienced firsthand the harm that occurs when dignity isn't prioritized. So, as a teacher returning to the classroom, what if she could cultivate a classroom where honoring dignity was embedded in the ecosystem?

Like many educators, Summer initially thought she already knew what dignity meant. She had used the words "dignity" and "respect" interchangeably for years. To her, they meant politeness, good manners, and fairness. All things she valued.

But as she learned more, she realized that, yes, all those things matter. But dignity is different and works on a higher plane. And dignity is not the same as respect. Respect is earned, but dignity is inherent.[1] Students don't deserve to be treated with dignity because they are well-behaved, hardworking, or compliant. They deserve it because they exist. This shift changed everything. She needed to keep learning.

So, around that time, she led a book study on *Dignity: Its Essential Role in Resolving Conflict* by Donna Hicks (2011), an international conflict-resolution specialist who argued that people need to be treated with dignity to be at their best. Donna offered practical tools for applying dignity to leadership, relationships, and conflict. The ideas resonated deeply with Summer. Simultaneously, she engaged in ongoing conversations with her supervisor, Floyd Cobb, about the role of dignity in education. Through him, she met John Krownapple. Those two became her support system for learning how to teach with dignity.

Everything was falling into place for Summer. She now had the concepts, language, tools, and support to center dignity in her own life and share it with others. Returning to the classroom, she no longer felt exhausted and powerless. Instead of trying to control every challenge, she focused on creating conditions where students could fully engage.

She tended her classroom like a gardener, knowing that flourishing depended on nurturing what lay beneath the surface. Dignity was the foundation, the soil where everything else would take root. She centered every choice and action on her students' innate worth, ensuring they had what they needed to grow. She resisted seeing them through the lens of deficit. They weren't problems to fix. They were people to cultivate.

---

1. Realizing this difference feels like finding out Fabrice Morvan and Rob Pilatus, better known as Milli Vanilli, weren't actually singers, but were just models lip-syncing to someone else's vocals. Mind blown.

The more she learned how to teach with dignity, the clearer things became: She wasn't fixing things; she was cultivating possibilities. But she also began wondering: If focusing on dignity made such a difference in her one classroom, why wasn't focusing on dignity already embedded in schools and classrooms everywhere?

Summer's question extends beyond her classroom and points to a deep and troubling issue with educational systems worldwide. But to understand why educators so often overlook dignity, we need to look beyond schools and those who work in them. We must examine the systems within which the schools, teachers, and students exist.

Dignity Is What's Missing

We (John and Floyd) supported Summer through this transition. Over the years, we've pondered the same question she found herself asking: Why isn't dignity embedded as the foundation of all classroom activity? Teaching based on dignity works because dignity is central to human nature. It works everywhere there are human beings. And yet, since the 1980s, most education systems[2] have prioritized accountability, efficiency, and standardization over human connections, ironically minimizing what makes meaningful learning possible (Starr, 2022).

However, we've seen countless educational policies and mission statements that imply dignity is valued ("We believe all students will achieve" and so on). Still, in practice, real-life recognition and valuing of dignity remain inconsistent. The presence of dignity in curriculum, instruction, and school culture is generally the exception, not the rule.

---

2. Finland stands out as a notable exception. While much of the world began reshaping education around standardized testing and top-down accountability in the 1980s, Finland charted a different course. Instead of high-stakes tests, they leaned into trust, fairness, and teacher autonomy. Think *Mr. Rogers' Neighborhood* meets education: calm, dignified, and completely uninterested in chasing test scores as if they were Pac-Man dots.

We continue to echo Summer's question: If dignity is essential—and we know that honoring dignity is vital for effective learning—why isn't it foundational in schools? Why isn't it talked about and planned for explicitly? To find an answer, we must take a broader historical and geographical view. How has dignity been positioned over time? How do different nations, institutions, and cultures currently incorporate it in schools?

With that context in mind, educators and stakeholders are better positioned to answer the most immediate and urgent question: How do teachers bring dignity to the forefront of their classrooms?

Positioning Dignity in the Global Education Context

Many parts of the world regard education as a fundamental human right. Global commitments such as the *Universal Declaration of Human Rights* (United Nations, 1948) and the *Convention on the Rights of the Child* (United Nations, 1989) affirm that every child has the right to a quality education. Education is seen as a right. But why?

The belief that every child has the right to a quality education is rooted in dignity, the inherent worth of every person. The European Union (2012) explicitly reinforces this connection in Article 1 of the EU Charter of Fundamental Rights, stating, "Human dignity is inviolable. It must be respected and protected." The protection of inviolable dignity applies just as much to education as it does to any other human right. The conviction that educators should teach, support, and treat students as whole persons shows a fundamental belief in their dignity.

Many nations, regions, and institutions have incorporated dignity-related ideas into their educational systems. For instance, legal protections in the United States, Indigenous reconciliation efforts in Canada and Australia, place-based learning in Hawai'i, universal access policies in Scandinavia, and the mission statements of independent and international schools all reflect a shared commitment to treating every student as worthy of an education. (For more examples of global efforts, see Appendix A.)

Yet the need to honor dignity is often lost in the everyday reality of schools. It's not unusual for classrooms to focus more on compliance than connection, which ends up reducing students to data points rather than treating them as whole learners. The issue isn't a lack of noble, humanistic ideals, but rather the difficulty of applying the ideals effectively within unsupportive systems.

The Why of Dignity: The Missing Piece in Education

It's not that educators don't care about human dignity. They do. We do! However, teachers work within educational systems shaped by logic that centers other priorities. In these environments, it's difficult for educators to know what dignity-honoring behaviors look like in practice. They're so seldom seen! Recognizing them is what Summer committed to learning.

Initially, she assumed teaching with dignity was about being nice, helping students feel happy, and being polite and respectful. While partially true, her assumptions were undeveloped. As Summer delved deeper, she realized that honoring dignity was a much more expansive idea. It wasn't about constantly feeling positive or ensuring students got what they wanted. Instead, honoring dignity involves treating people as inherently valuable and worthy. It's a mindset. Thus, teaching with dignity requires a noncontrolling and humble attitude, a willingness to acknowledge mistakes, an assumption of goodwill, and a celebration of growth.

Dignity (an innate state) isn't a prize for students to win; they already possess it. Every human being does. Unlike respect (a temporary feeling), dignity is nonnegotiable. It's innate. Yet, in schools, dignity often takes a backseat to performance. In pursuit of it, modern education systems tend to suppress meaningful human connection, prioritizing compliance instead. Priorities like standardized behaviors, rigid discipline policies, uniform curriculum pacing, and high-stakes assessments can influence educators to unintentionally overlook dignity even when they are using the most human-centered strategies, which renders the strategies ineffective.

Defining Dignity in Action

So, what exactly is dignity? International affairs and conflict-resolution expert Dr. Donna Hicks (2011, 2018) defines it as the inherent value and worth of every person; she warns that dignity is easily ignored or undermined. Her research demonstrates that honoring dignity transforms relationships, institutions, communities, and, yes, even classrooms. When teachers treat themselves and their students with dignity, their classroom environments become more supportive. Teachers experience greater well-being, and students feel safer. A feeling of safety fosters belonging, which increases engagement, a foundational element of learning and achievement (Freeman et al., 2014).

What does it look like to treat a student with dignity? How do teachers honor dignity in real, everyday moments? Drawing from years of conflict resolution and research, Donna identified the essential human needs that, when met, help people feel valued. Her Dignity Model and its 10 Essential Elements of Dignity (Table 1.1) offer educators a starting point for answering the question of what dignity in action looks like.

Students feel valued, capable, and connected when they experience dignity (the behaviors, attitudes, and assumptions that Donna calls the 10 Essential Elements of Dignity) in their classrooms. When these elements are missing, the impact is predictable: Engagement and achievement suffer. Students may disengage, act out, or struggle to learn. From behavioral issues to lack of motivation, persistent challenges are signs that the educational system has compromised dignity. These problems aren't simply discipline problems or achievement gaps.

TABLE 1.1

Donna Hicks's 10 Essential Elements of Dignity

Essential Need	Description of Action to Meet the Need
Independence	Enable people to act for themselves, fostering control, hope, and possibility.
Benefit of the Doubt	Treat people with the assumption that they act with integrity and good intent.
Understanding	Show that others' perspectives matter by listening and seeking to understand.
Safety	Work to ensure physical and psychological security, free from harm, shame, or humiliation.
Inclusion	Help others feel they belong in all aspects of a relationship or community.
Acknowledgment	Fully listen, validate, and respond to people's experiences.
Accountability	Own your actions, apologize, and commit to change.
Fairness	Treat others justly according to shared principles.
Acceptance of Identity	Honor people as they are without judgment or superiority.
Recognition	Appreciate others' contributions, talents, and efforts, offering praise generously.

Note: Summary of concepts based on Hicks, 2018.

To recap, the problem isn't rooted in teacher intentions, dedication, or ability. The real problem is that, for four decades, the typical structure of educational systems—especially those shaped by high-stakes account-ability—has prioritized compliance over connection and growth. This is where the problem of misimplementation comes in.

Misimplementation and Its Evil Twin: Deficit Thinking

Misimplementation is widespread in the field of education. It occurs when a program or strategy is applied incorrectly or inconsistently, thus reducing effectiveness or leading to unintended consequences. Too often, well-intended instructional strategies fail because educators implement them without adhering to their human-centered design or purpose. In other words, honoring dignity was in the intent but got lost in the application.

When compliance takes precedence over human connection, even re-search-backed approaches become hollow. And remember that most educational systems are set up to prioritize compliance. When compliance rather than dignity is the main goal, it reduces teaching to task completion, box-checking, and mandate enforcement rather than meaningful learning. As Kirsten Olson (2009) documents in *Wounded by School*, many students experience schooling as a process of correction and control rather than one of curiosity and growth. Over time, this emphasis on compliance erodes confidence, creativity, and intrinsic motivation. Without dignity at the center, instructional methods feel like obligations rather than opportunities to foster belonging and engagement.

This dignity gap explains why efforts to improve student achievement so often fall short. They ignore a deeper issue: the absence of dignity-centered practices and policies within the system. From the United States to the United Kingdom, from Australia to parts of Africa, Asia, and beyond, the pervasive influence of neoliberal education philosophy (and its underlying economic worldview) has emphasized accountability, data, and measurable outcomes over the human experience in school.[3] For decades, this logic has shaped systems worldwide and often conditions teachers—who frequently don't realize it—to see students for what they lack and to act as problem solvers of student deficits instead of seeing students for what they bring and to act like facilitators of student growth.

This mindset, known as deficit thinking, frames student struggles as personal shortcomings rather than reflections of their learning conditions (Valencia, 1997). Instead of recognizing students as capable learners navigating complex challenges, deficit thinking positions them as problems that need fixing. Within this frame, schools function to correct students rather than to cultivate students' potential.

Even widely accepted human-centered educational frameworks such as cooperative learning, multicultural education, differentiated instruction, culturally responsive teaching, and Universal Design for Learning can fall into the trap of being perceived as tools to fix students. Too often, they become structured checklists instead of transformative tools. Instead of fostering connection, they reinforce compliance. Instead of enabling agency, they reduce learning to task mechanical execution. (For a summary of research on instructional misimplementation, see Appendix B.)

Deficit Thinking in a Post-Pandemic World

Of course, deficit thinking isn't new, but the 2020 pandemic made it worse, fast. The aftermath of this disruption to schooling pushed educators into survival mode, enabling a perpetual fix-the-problem mindset and creating a near-constant state of triage (see Appendix C):

---

3. Neoliberal education philosophy started to take root in the 1980s alongside leg warmers and the rise of personal computing. It emphasizes market-driven values like accountability, competition, and measurable outcomes. While those aims aren't inherently bad, they can go sideways when compliance and control crowd out connection, creativity, and care. We're not saying toss the spreadsheets. Just don't forget the keep the focus on students.

- **Learning loss** rhetoric framed students as broken rather than resilient.
- Escalating **behavioral challenges** reinforced deficit-based discipline.
- A growing **mental health crisis** overwhelmed schools, which were never equipped to address it.
- Widespread **disengagement and absenteeism** made many teachers question whether they were truly reaching their students.
- Rising **public mistrust** fueled division instead of partnership.
- **Teacher burnout** made it harder to maintain a strengths-based perspective.

It's easy for deficit thinking to take hold in an environment where problem after problem pops up,[4] trapping educators in a cycle of seeing students for what's missing rather than for what's possible.

Dignity as the Solution: Teaching with a New Mindset

At the beginning of this chapter, we invited you to join us in imagining a better way of teaching. Imagine education built on dignity. Teachers would focus on creating conditions to help students thrive instead of being shoehorned into trying to fix their apparent deficits. Educators would not obsessively correct behaviors; instead, they would first address what's beneath the undesirable behavior. Instead of seeing a struggling student as a problem to manage, the student would be seen as a learner to support. Imagine what schools could achieve if they were run on such a system!

Consider a student sitting at a desk, shoulders slumped, staring blankly

---

4. Teaching post-pandemic can feel like an endless game of Whac-A-Mole. Just swap the rubber mallet for paperwork and emotional exhaustion. But dignity reminds us: We don't have to chase every problem. We can change the game.

at an assignment. He seems sullen. This student never asks a question and never raises a hand. His assignments are late and incomplete when he does hand them in. Maybe one day he erupts in angry behavior. Or, perhaps, his will to even try simply ebbs away. In that case, he may stop coming to school.

The educational system conditions teachers to see behavior problems, period. Various checklists might categorize this student as defiant, disengaged, or inattentive. Policies might prescribe punitive consequences such as detentions. But what if the real issue isn't the student at all? What if these behaviors are symptoms of a more profound experience of not feeling seen, valued, or worthy?

As Alfie Kohn (1996) argued in *Beyond Discipline: From Compliance to Community*, discipline systems fail students because they assume behavior management is about exerting control rather than creating an environment where students feel intrinsically motivated to engage. If that's the case, then misbehavior isn't the problem. The real issue is the absence of a dignity-centered environment.

Beyond Specific Instructional Strategies

Teaching with dignity is not about using any single strategy or following one prescribed method. It's about implementing whatever strategies you choose in a way that honors students' dignity rather than reducing learning to compliance. Depending on how it's implemented, a teaching strategy can foster connection and deep learning or become another empty routine from which students (and teachers) disengage.

If you've been in education for a while, chances are you've encountered promising instructional methods that fell flat in practice. Perhaps you found them frustrating or ineffective. Many teachers abandon well-known methods of instruction when they don't perform as they were supposed to.

In these cases, the problem is usually misimplementation. The fact is that how a method is implemented matters more than the method itself. Let's look at a strategy with enormous potential that is often misused and then falls out of favor: the Jigsaw Method. This approach has an extraordinarily high impact on student achievement when it's done well. Ironically, it's also one of the most frequently misimplemented instructional strategies within the field of education.

If you've struggled with Jigsaw in the past, you're not alone. Many teachers eventually abandon it. The strategy isn't flawed, however; the real issue is a deeper structural misalignment. Jigsaw is a human-centered approach, yet most educational systems operate through a compliance-centered logic. As a result, many educators haven't seen Jigsaw implemented in a way that works. But research consistently shows that it yields impressive results when implemented with integrity. That's why we're using it as an illustrative example: to show how dignity-centered implementation unlocks its full potential and what can happen when it's missing.

Case Study: The Jigsaw Method

In teacher prep, you likely learned about the Jigsaw Method (Aronson et al., 1978), but you may not know its backstory. Many educators don't. Hang in there while we share some history. It's interesting and enlightening.

In 1971, Elliot Aronson and his team from the University of Texas at Austin developed Jigsaw in response to racial tensions. The city's newly deseg-regated schools were hostile environments, sometimes escalating into violence. Students from marginalized social groups were often treated as less worthy of opportunity and respect.

The Jigsaw Method disrupted the traditional classroom environment that positioned students as rivals. Aronson's strategy ensured that every student could meaningfully contribute to the group's learning process.

Jigsaw positioned students as peers and collaborators so that students could recognize each other's competence. Social hierarchies faded into nonrelevance as the students became resources for each other's success. Each student was an important piece of the jigsaw puzzle.

More than an innovative strategy, Jigsaw was a brilliant intervention in a system (and society) that had yet to ensure every child was equally seen, heard, and valued. The idea was simple:

- Each student became an expert in a part of the lesson.
- That student then taught their part to their peers, making every student's role essential.

Before long, Jigsaw classrooms became increasingly cohesive, safe, and supportive. Students who had ignored or antagonized each other began working together, engaging deeply, and valuing one another. Early trials deemed the strategy a huge success.

Long-term studies confirmed these effects. Jigsaw classrooms reduced racial hostility, increased harmony, and led to measurable academic gains, especially for students in historically marginalized groups. Decades later, John Hattie's (2023) synthesis of research meta-analyses reaffirmed its success, showing an effect size of 1.20, which is usually interpreted as 3 years' worth of growth in 1 school year.[5]

---

5. If education had a stock market, Jigsaw would be like buying Apple in the 1980s. Too bad two of these authors were too busy with baseball cards, BMX bikes, and *Star Wars* to learn how to invest in stocks. Summer was also busy, listening to Casey Kasem's *American Top 40*, hyper-focused on pressing the record button on her cassette deck at just the right time.

Case Study: Common Pitfalls of Misimplementation

Despite its potential, Jigsaw is often misused, diluted, and ineffective. Instead of fostering positive interdependence and individual accountability, misimplementation reduces Jigsaw to a mechanical exercise, stripping away its effectiveness (Buchs et al., 2023; Montazeri et al., 2022). Without dignity explicitly at the center, Jigsaw can become just one more exercise in compliance and ticking boxes.

The following statements describe some of Jigsaw's more common pitfalls and how misimplementation neglects the Essential Elements of Dignity (Table 1.1).

- **Rushed Expert Groups** → Students skim information rather than engage deeply, undermining dignity needs such as safety, independence, and understanding.

- **Unstructured Peer Teaching** → Dominant voices take over, and others disengage, violating needs such as inclusion, fairness, and accountability.

- **Lack of Reflection** → Learning becomes superficial rather than meaningful, neglecting essentials like the benefit of the doubt and recognition.

Without careful implementation, Jigsaw shifts from being a tool for connection to just another mundane classroom task. When students don't feel their contributions matter, the impact is lost, and Jigsaw fails to bridge academic gaps and social divisions.

Jigsaw's effectiveness is due to something more than its structure and steps. The whole is greater than the sum of the parts. It works when teachers prioritize dignity within the Jigsaw structure. This recognition of students' innate dignity calls forth their engagement and best efforts. The learning process becomes alive. When Jigsaw and other strategies are applied in this way, they create meaningful learning experiences. But, too often, execution becomes the goal rather than a means to something deeper.[6]

This pattern of neglecting dignity extends beyond Jigsaw. Many instructional methods initially designed to foster connection, engagement, and agency lose their impact when reduced to rigid checklists. The difference lies in how methods are applied (Table 1.2). Are the strategies used as mechanical procedures? Or as opportunities to affirm students' worth, foster connection, and catalyze authentic engagement?

TABLE 1.2

Comparison of Approaches to Implementation

Mechanical Implementation	Relational Implementation
What steps must I take when using Jigsaw as a teaching strategy?	How do I honor my students' dignity and foster meaningful learning through Jigsaw?
I need to try Jigsaw because research says it improves outcomes.	I value student agency and independence, and Jigsaw helps me act on those values.
How can I get students to follow the Jigsaw protocol?	How can students partner with each other and perceive each other as competent?

Even within systems that often set educators up for misimplementation, teachers still have the power to bring good theories to life with intention. A single shift in mindset can make all the difference:

---

6. A mentor of John's once told him that Jigsaw is the opposite of pizza. Good pizza is great, and bad pizza is still decent (after all, it's pizza). But Jigsaw? When done well, it's the best thing we could be doing. When done poorly, let's just say, nobody is coming back for seconds...ever. Turns out the missing ingredient is dignity, not sardines.

✕	✓
"How do I implement this theory correctly?"	"How does this theory help me honor my students' innate value and worth?"

When dignity becomes the foundation of teaching, pedagogy becomes authentic, students feel valued, and teachers regain a sense of purpose that extends far beyond fixing problems.

Case Study: Implementation with Dignity

At its core, Jigsaw ensures every student plays an essential role in learning. But for it to work, dignity must be embedded in every step:

1. **Divide the Class into Home Groups.** → Students expect to collaborate.

2. **Assign Each Student a Unique Piece of Content.** → Every student within a Home Group gains a piece of knowledge essential to the group's task (subtopic).

3. **Form Expert Groups.** → Students collaborate with peers from other groups to deepen their knowledge of the assigned subtopic.

4. **Return to Home Groups and Teach.** → Students share their expertise with their peers.

5. **Synthesize and Assess Learning.** → The group pieces everything together.

For Jigsaw (and any other well-designed teaching approach) to fulfill its purpose, dignity must remain at the core during implementation:

- Each student must feel that their contribution is essential, not just obligatory.

- Collaboration must feel purposeful, not just procedural.[7]
- Teachers must guide and enable student self-empowerment, agency, and ownership. They must not micromanage.

When dignity is the guiding principle, Jigsaw transcends mechanics and delivers on its promise. It both leads to academic gains and sustains a classroom environment where students feel accepted, validated, appreciated, and deeply connected.

Beyond Jigsaw: Teaching with Dignity in Any Method

There's no doubt about it: Jigsaw works best when implemented with dignity. But dignity isn't just another strategy. It's also a mindset. It's how we think about our students. It's the foundation that makes all strategies meaningful. What matters isn't which approach is used but how an approach is implemented. Pretty much all approaches can work well when they're implemented with the mindset that assumes the dignity of each student.

Since dignity makes Jigsaw effective, what would happen if we embedded dignity across all our instructional approaches? What if every teaching method—whether direct instruction, inquiry-based learning, or project-based learning—was implemented with the commitment to honoring dignity?

Beyond instruction, what if dignity shaped every dimension of classroom life: the structure of routines, the response to challenges, the design of assessments, and so on?

Embedding dignity is the next step in transforming education.

---

7. Just ask *The Goonies*, a group of kids from a 1985 adventure film who stumble into an underground treasure hunt. True teamwork isn't about holding hands and following a map; it's about figuring things out together, even if it means dodging booby traps and outwitting a notorious family of criminals.

Bringing Dignity to Teaching

Dignity isn't just an instructional mindset. It's also a broad principle that can influence every interaction, decision, and practice in the classroom.[8] When it becomes the foundation of teacher planning and preparation, instruction, relationships, classroom culture, and professional responsibilities, students experience an environment where they truly are valued.

Since we've already explored Jigsaw as a model (although there are other noteworthy examples we could have chosen), let's analyze how it works when aligned with dignity. When properly implemented, Jigsaw meets essential human needs for dignity, such as the following:

- **Independence** → Students take ownership of their learning.
- **Recognition** → Their contributions are vital to the group's success.
- **Fairness** → The task of learning is equally and justly shared.
- **Understanding** → Students listen to learn and engage with other perspectives.

Of course, these elements are not Jigsaw-specific; they're universal. They represent the values that educators must actively protect and sustain to prevent any instructional approach from being absorbed into a system's compliance-driven logic. Any strategy that honors dignity can deepen engagement, build trust, and support meaningful learning.

Dignity-centered teaching isn't about choosing one method; it's about intentionally approaching every technique, every moment, and every

---

8. If this seems overwhelming, Kimberly Strong, one of our partners from Central Oregon, has a suggestion: Think of it as training for a marathon and building stamina over time. So, with dignity, start small and strengthen the habit; it's all about progress. It's kind of like learning to solve a Rubik's Cube: At first, it's hard and slow, but with practice, you get faster...unless you're still peeling off the stickers, which ends up ruining it. Remember: No shortcuts!

interaction with dignity in mind. Whether through classroom discussions, grading policies, or behavioral expectations, dignity can be the common thread that connects them all and leads to better results.

Take a moment (perhaps with a colleague) to reflect on these questions:

- Which dignity essentials are already present in your teaching?
- Which need more intentional reinforcement?
- How might dignity guide not just your instructional choices but also how you structure your entire learning environment?

When we move beyond mechanics and embrace dignity as the driving force behind all aspects of teaching, education becomes more than a collection of strategies. It becomes a comprehensive experience that honors students as whole persons.

That is the true power of teaching with dignity.

From Fixing Problems to Cultivating Growth

Entering this profession includes adopting the fundamental role of a nurturer who helps students grow and develop. Yet, too often, teaching feels like a never-ending uphill battle, like tackling 10 jobs simultaneously with fewer and fewer resources.

Or, to use a gardening analogy[9] (more on this later), it can feel like battling relentless weeds. Instead of cultivating curiosity, the focus remains fixed on tracking deficits. Instead of fostering growth, the pressure is to pull up every problem (or weed) before it spreads. But no matter how much effort goes into clearing the garden patch, new weeds appear. Then the system reinforces itself: more interventions, more assessments, and even

---

9. A gardening metaphor? In an education book? Groundbreaking! (See what we did there?)

more sweeping initiatives designed to eliminate problems, whether those problems exist within the system, the world, or the students themselves.

But here's the fundamental shift: Teaching with dignity isn't about fixing students; it's about working with students to create conditions where they can thrive. Dignity is the missing piece within education systems. More than a feel-good ideal, dignity provides an essential framework for learning and growth. When honored, dignity helps students feel a sense of belonging and develop confidence in their ability to achieve. When dignity is neglected, however, motivation declines, behavior challenges rise, and systems remain centered on (or revert to) control and compliance over connection.

It's easy to fall into the trap of reactive thinking; negativity is powerful. The instinct to fix problems as quickly as possible feels productive, yet it often leads to a constant state of reaction. Fixing should be reserved for true emergencies. The real personal and collective challenge is to break free from negative thinking and sustain a new normal. The next chapter will explore how to overcome the negative mindset.

To transform the classroom experience (for teachers and students), teaching must shift from reacting to problems toward responding to people. This remains an ongoing challenge regardless of the setting or where educators are in their careers. The key is to develop the ability to cultivate a dignity-centered classroom environment, just as master gardeners build knowledge and skills to sustain rich and supportive ecosystems.[10]

So grab your gardening tools. Let's dig in.

---

10. And not like us, fumbling with houseplants and overwatering succulents into oblivion. RIP to the ones we've lost.

CHAPTER 2

Our Approach: Thinking Like A Dignity Gardener

Darkness cannot drive out darkness; only light can do that.
Hate cannot drive out hate; only love can do that.

—Dr. Martin Luther King Jr., 1963

Got Your Tools? Ready to Dig In?

How educators think about teaching influences everything: their choices, classroom environments, and responses to students. Most teachers enter the profession to cultivate growth, much like gardeners. However, typical education systems draw their attention to deficiencies, encouraging them to control behaviors and eliminate problems rather than foster success.

This negative mindset shift happens quietly, but it changes everything. A struggling student becomes a disruption to manage rather than a learner to support. A disengaged student becomes someone to correct rather than reconnect with. Over time, reacting to problems replaces the work of building something better. But we invite you to imagine another way. Instead of defining teaching success by fixing issues, imagine measuring it by the presence of healthy conditions and thriving students.

Before discussing how to make that dream a reality, we'll explain how negative framing traps educators in reaction cycles and why shifting toward a solution-focused mindset is the key to lasting change. This chapter focuses on this topic. We'll begin with Summer Synder's experiences after she received the Teacher of the Year Award.

Forget quick fixes. Forget checklists. Let's dig in.

Summer's Reflections

Summer's award day passed in a happy blur. When she showed her students her award plaque, they almost burst with pride. Later that evening, she collapsed onto her couch at home, exhaustion and exhilaration tangled together, the cheers of her colleagues still ringing in her head.

Her phone buzzed. She'd received many congratulatory texts from friends, family, and colleagues. She'd also reached out to a fair number of people. But there were two people she hadn't shared her news with yet: Floyd Cobb and John Krownapple, her primary supporters for learning how to teach with dignity.

With a satisfied sigh, she picked up her phone and opened their group text thread, affectionately named *Dignity Dream Team*.

Summer

> Big news, guys! Guess who's Teacher of the Year?!

She attached a picture of herself holding the bouquet from the ceremony, her daughters beaming beside her. The reply dots popped up immediately.

Floyd

Wow! Huge congrats, Summer!
Well deserved. Can we officially call
you "Dr. Dignity" now?

John

Teacher of the Year? More like
Teacher of the Century!

Summer smiled as she typed back.

Summer

Thanks, guys. I owe a big part of this to you two. Your
ideas kept me grounded this year. Every day felt like
planting seeds and waiting to see what would grow.

Floyd's response made her pause.

Floyd

What do you think was your biggest
challenge this year?

*She smiled and shook her head. Just like Floyd to ask
such a reflective question. So much had shifted. How
could she sum it up?*

Summer

It's my thinking, for sure. I used to fixate on problems like gaps, behaviors, and what needed fixing. But this year, I stopped micromanaging and started focusing on creating the right conditions. Like in my garden, I can't rush my pansies to grow. All I can do is provide sunlight, water, and good soil. It's the same in the classroom. Set up the right environment and trust the process.

She hit send and leaned back, exhaling.

John

That's beautiful, Summer. And it reminds me of something I've been working on—a little fable about teaching and gardening. Sending it your way now.

A moment later, John's document arrived on Summer's phone.

She began to read.

The Gardener and the Pest Exterminator

Once upon a time, an old Gardener sold fruits and vegetables at the market in a small village. Her produce was far from perfect: crooked carrots, bumpy apples, misshapen potatoes. But the villagers didn't care. Her fruit might look ugly, but it tasted good.

One day, a traveling Pest Exterminator arrived. He was full of the latest theories about pest control. He cried out to the villagers: "These deformed crops suffer from a pest infestation! Apples should be smooth! Carrots should be straight! But do not fear. I will eliminate the Ugly Fruit Pest!"

The villagers exchanged skeptical glances as the Exterminator rattled off a list of poisons that no one could pronounce. He promised a perfect harvest the following year.

"Come back to me then, and you'll see the difference!" he declared, eyeing the old Gardener. She took a bite of a bumpy apple and shrugged.

During the growing season, the Gardener worked as usual: tended the soil, balanced the minerals, and trusted the plants to grow in their own ways. She used natural solutions for pests and believed that healthy crops didn't need constant intervention.

Meanwhile, the Exterminator waged war, spraying, trapping, and treating everything that moved. He even developed a rash from an accidental chemical spill.

"Occupational hazard," he muttered.

The next year, market days came around again. The Exterminator's stall was dazzling: brightly painted, lights blinking, and pristine displays. "No Ugly Fruit!" his sign boasted. Identical oval potatoes were lined up like soldiers. His apples rose in uniform pyramids. But when the villagers took a bite, their faces fell.

"It's...tasteless."

Meanwhile, the Gardener's gnarled carrots and misshapen pears burst with flavor. People flocked to her stall, leaving the Exterminator's perfect-but-bland produce behind.

The Exterminator fumed and muttered that his theories had been published and were all the rage among exterminators. But the proof was in the pudding. Despite his dedication to anti-problem theories and even despite his good intentions, his perfect fruits and vegetables, sprayed to within an inch of their lives, hadn't developed. They were bitter, sour, and tasteless.

The End.

Summer laughed out loud. Then she read the story again. She used to be that Pest Exterminator, but now she was the Gardener.

The Trap of Negative Thinking

Negative thinking is seductive. It lures individuals into its trap with a false sense of control, much like bait on a hook. Once folks bite, they're trapped in reaction mode.

Consider the Pest Exterminator who fell into this trap despite well-intentioned enthusiasm. He didn't know any better but—and this is truly unfortunate but happens all the time with educators and administrators—he thought he knew better. In fact, he was convinced he knew best. He fixated on threats, believing extermination was the only solution. He waged a relentless war on weeds and bugs but neglected to nurture the soil.

Once you see the flaw in this approach, it's hard to ignore. Education systems often condition teachers to fixate on and eliminate problems. Issues like low test scores, classroom disruptions, disengagement, and undesired behaviors quickly become perceived threats demanding control. This results in more intervention, remediation, and compliance, leading educators to neglect the crucial task of fostering the essential conditions that support student success.

The urgency of exterminating problems makes negative thinking hard to overcome. While sometimes necessary, this mindset emphasizes elimination over growth. But this negative thinking isn't merely a bad habit; it's also ingrained in human psychology. The brain prioritizes threats as a survival mechanism. Negative experiences linger longer than positive ones, negative emotions hit harder, and failures feel more pressing than successes (Cacioppo et al., 2014; Gottman & Levenson, 2002; Ito et al., 1998; Kahneman & Tversky, 1984).

As *Star Wars* villain Darth Vader[11] once warned, "You underestimate the power of the Dark Side" (Marquand, 1983). His insight is relevant here; negative thinking holds significant power. It commands attention, fuels adrenaline, spawns quick reactions, and can mislead educators into believing that fixing problems equates to achieving success.

However, no garden flourishes by waging war on weeds. You don't foster thriving students by simply eliminating problems (especially when the system frames the students themselves as the problem).

So why are educators likely to reach for pesticide spray bottles filled with negative thinking rather than watering cans brimming with positive thoughts?[12] Beyond systemic factors that promote this mindset, negative thinking is simply easier. As *Star Wars* hero Yoda (small, green, and wise) explained, "[The Dark Side] is quicker, easier, more seductive" (Kershner, 1980).

And therein lies the real danger: reacting negatively and dismantling problems is more straightforward than the disciplined work of responding deliberately and building solutions. Though flourishing classrooms aren't built on negative reactions and motivations (such as fear or self-assertion), these ineffective approaches have become the norm—or, you might say, the default.

Rocky Soil: Anti-Problem Thinking

Negative thinking shapes perspectives and entire systems. When schools prioritize fixing students over fostering growth, it influences everything.

- Discipline policies prioritize punishment over connection.

---

11. Darth Vader? In the middle of a gardening metaphor? We're children of the 1980s. Please forgive us.

12. Not that we're judging. If you've ever seen us try to keep a houseplant alive, you'd know that we're good with metaphors but not the actual gardening part.

- Struggling students are labeled as being at-risk rather than full of potential.
- School improvement efforts focus on gaps rather than on cultivating strengths.

It's like a gardener who relentlessly sprays pesticides but never checks the soil composition for minerals that fuel plant growth; incidentally, healthy soil also offers a good deal of natural protection against pests. Education systems condition teachers to treat symptoms instead of causes, leading to an endless cycle of behavior plans, remediation, and interventions. We call this anti-problem thinking.

It's worth repeating that, to the human biological nervous system, being anti-problem feels right. Negative thinking is instinctual; it's our survival hardwiring. Early humans scanned for predators; today, educators scan for problems. Instead of tigers, they scan for gaps, low test scores, disengagement, and disruptions.

Once people label something as a problem, it becomes easy to spend time and energy—sometimes a lot of time and energy—analyzing, dissecting, and holding meetings about it without solving it. No wonder many school improvement efforts feel like an endless loop of admiring the problem (Senge, 1990).

But admiring the problem is not the only way schools get stuck. The other way? Trying to fix their way to success without creating the conditions for success.

- A district that becomes hyper-focused on reducing disciplinary infractions may impose harsher punishments, which will only increase student resentment and disengagement.
- A system obsessed with preventing failure may ignore academic challenges, unintentionally weakening students' ability to persist and learn.

Why Anti-Problem Thinking Feels Right—But Goes Wrong

It seems responsible for people to fix problems, but eliminating a negative is not the same as creating a positive.

- Efforts to eliminate exclusion don't always create belonging.
- Policies designed to prevent failure don't necessarily foster resilience.
- Anti-bullying campaigns don't automatically build a culture of kindness.

This thinking pattern highlights the fundamental flaw of anti-problem thinking and tricks people into believing faulty logic: If they fix enough problems, students will thrive.

But history proves otherwise. For instance, the war on drugs during the 1980s in the United States criminalized addiction without addressing root causes, leaving communities worse off.[13] Likewise, some anti-bullying programs have backfired, unintentionally reinforcing aggressive behaviors by modeling what not to do rather than what to do.

Yet, when these efforts fail, some people dig in their heels and double down on the approach. This is because anti-problem thinking can shape identities, and not just reactions.

Consider, for example, a teacher who builds her professional identity around fighting unfairness. The stronger she builds this identity, the more

---

13. Ah, the 1980s, when the war on drugs was in full swing, synth-pop ruled the airwaves, and Saturday mornings were sacred (that's when the best cartoons aired). We were told to "Just Say No," yet somehow no one said no to neon-colored spandex, perms, or the countless number of movies about kids befriending aliens. Simpler times? Maybe. But let's be real: If solving problems were as easy as an after-school public service announcement (PSA), we wouldn't still be having this conversation.

she must ignore the unspoken question: "If unfairness were fixed and eliminated, who would I be? Maybe I'd be a nobody." This question can be so unsettling as to constitute an existential threat. Since the nervous system promotes safety by identifying and eliminating threats (both external and internal), it must react to this tacit identity crisis. Directly confronting it would create unsafety (discomfort, uncertainty, etc.), so the teacher subconsciously eliminates the threat through avoidance, intensifying her efforts to combat unfairness.

For many, staying in battle mode feels safer than pausing to ask what comes next. It's not just about eliminating unfairness but also proving they're among the good ones. The allure of moral superiority is powerful. It feels righteous, urgent, and deeply validating. But at some point, the fight should end. Right? The problem should be solved. What then? Here's the hard truth: A system designed to eliminate problems will always find more problems to eliminate. Why are we surprised? We shouldn't be.

This isn't speculation; it's backed by research. For instance, mandatory anti-prejudice training can fail to produce lasting behavioral change or even create backlash (Dobbin & Kalev, 2016; Duguid & Thomas-Hunt, 2015; Forscher et al., 2016; Legault et al., 2011). Despite good intentions, anti-problem approaches have inherent limitations that often lead to frustration, fatigue, failure, and backlash (Appendix D).

And if you don't believe us, believe Yoda.[14] He didn't encourage Luke Skywalker to be anti–Dark Side. He didn't say, "Dedicate yourself to eradicating Sith Lords." Instead, he urged him to embrace the Light Side—to

---

14. Yes, we did it again. If this book had a soundtrack, it'd be playing *Man in the Mirror* while we sip Capri Suns, tuck the manuscript into our Trapper Keepers, and debate whether *The Empire Strikes Back* or *Back to the Future* is the greatest movie of all time. The Force of childhood nostalgia is strong with us.

build rather than merely resist.

The Perfect Storm: System + Cognition = Harm

Anti-problem thinking isn't just a habit. It's also a (bad) habit reinforced by the perfect storm: education systems that prioritize problem elimination, and human brains wired to detect and respond to threats. Together, these condition educators to fix, fix, fix students.

- Low test scores? Threat to school accountability and teacher competence.
- Student misbehavior? Threat to classroom order and management skills.
- Engagement drop? Threat to instructional effectiveness.

At every level of the system—curriculum standards, assessment frameworks, and accountability measures—education tends to focus on detecting, diagnosing, and diminishing problems. When the system rewards problem-spotting and teachers are neurologically primed to react to perceived threats, it's no wonder the default reaction to problems is to ask, "What's wrong with this student?"

This systemic obsession with fixing rather than fostering creates a vicious cycle of deficit thinking, harm, and squandered potential (Figure 2.1).

1. **Deficit Thinking Takes Hold.** Teachers learn to focus on gaps and what students lack rather than what they bring; the system frames students as problems to fix.

2. **Negative Thinking Is Amplified.** The brain's threat response kicks in, deficiencies feel urgent, and educators react with opposition to the problem.

3. **Educators React with Anti-Problem Strategies.** The urge to fix leads to punitive discipline, excessive remediation, rigid interventions, and so on.

4. **Actions Harm More Than Help.** Reactions stifle student growth. Students internalize that they are perceived as problems, not potential to be cultivated.

↻ **The Cycle Continues.** Undesirable student outcomes reinforce deficit thinking and the belief that students must be fixed rather than supported by their environment.[15]

FIGURE 2.1

The Vicious Cycle of Harmful Schooling

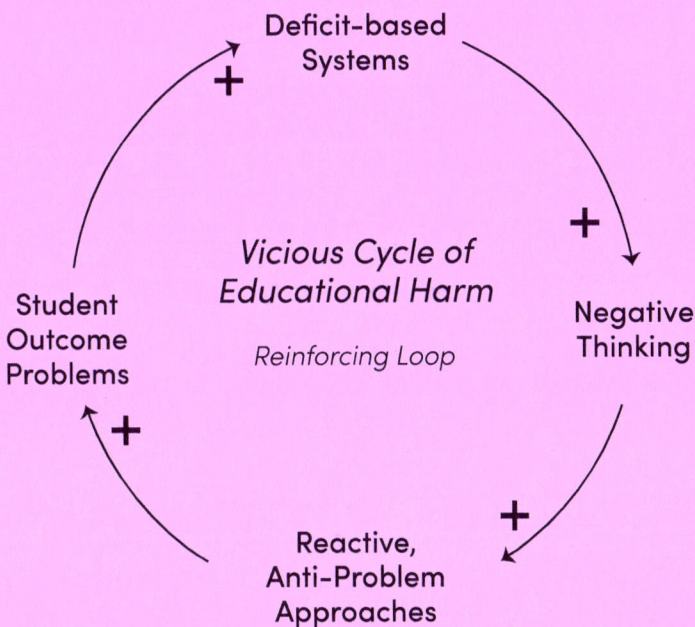

The Vicious Cycle Continues—Until We Break It

This cycle is frustrating and harmful. It exhausts educators, disengages

---

15. John can't resist a good Systems Thinking diagram. Left unchecked, you'd be looking at nothing but artfully tangled loops and arrows. Fortunately, Floyd reins it in with crisp, linear logic. Two minds, two maps. Welcome to our process.

students, and stifles innovation. Worst of all, it doesn't even work. For instance, consider the following:

- Punitive discipline leads to higher dropout rates (LiCalsi et al., 2021).
- Over-remediation weakens rather than builds students' confidence (Michigan Department of Education, 2021).
- Rigid accountability systems create more stress than success (Darling-Hammond et al., 2002).

At some point, we must ask ourselves, What if it's this reactive and rigid approach to problems that's keeping us stuck?

However, getting unstuck does not mean ignoring problems. It means changing the lens through which we see the issues. Consider these shifts in perspective:

- "How do we fix disengagement?" → "How will we increase connectedness?"
- "How do we stop failure?" → "How will we model resilience?"
- "How do we prevent misbehavior?" → "How will we foster belonging?"
- "How can we improve discipline?" → "How will we make accountability possible?"

The shift from anti-problem to pro-solution is more than semantics. It's transformational. Take the word "misbehavior," for example. The pressure to control student behavior often traps educators in reaction mode, reinforcing the very negative cycle they need to break. But what if there were a way to reinterpret student struggles?

Psychiatrist Daniel Siegel and child development expert Tina Payne Bryson (2011) offer a powerful reframe in *The Whole-Brain Child*: Instead of seeing a child as giving adults a hard time, see them as having a hard time. This subtle shift moves the adult from a reactive stance of control to a responsive stance of connection.

This general principle applies in the classroom. Rather than treating behavior as something to punish, teachers can view it as evidence of unmet needs. A defiant student may be frustrated or afraid, perhaps struggling with an assignment but too embarrassed to ask for help. A disengaged student may not be lazy but disconnected, possibly withdrawing because they don't feel valued.

This shift isn't just about perspective; it's also about practice. Seeing behavior as a signal rather than a disruption shifts teachers from reacting to problems to responding to needs, and it involves ditching the exterminator mindset in favor of something radically different: the gardener's approach.

Fertile Ground: Solution-Focused Thinking

Gardeners don't spend all their time pulling weeds. They primarily cultivate the soil so weeds don't take over in the first place. Solution-focused thinking does the same.

It shifts the question from **"What do we need to fix?"** to **"What's needed for growth that's missing?"**

Still, some might ask, "Isn't focusing on the solution just toxic positivity?" No. Toxic positivity ignores struggles and glosses over harm. Solution-focused thinking acknowledges problems but refuses to let them dictate the approach. It prioritizes creation over reaction, building over dismantling.

To clarify, here's what we're not saying:

∅ We are not ignoring injustice, harm, or inequity.

- ☑ We are not suggesting teachers should simply "think happy thoughts."
- ☑ We are not advocating for shallow, feel-good programs that avoid real change.
- ☑ And we are most definitely not saying the solution is to burn down the system.

We're simply saying that the most effective way to solve problems is to build something better, not just dismantle what's broken.

- ⊘ Anti-problem thinking keeps us stuck.
- ☑ Solution-focused thinking moves us forward.[16]

A Vision Rooted in Dignity

Shifting from anti-problem thinking to solution-focused teaching requires a mindset shift: Students are not problems to fix. They are persons with dignity and potential.

Although the primary issue is systems that reinforce deficit thinking, that doesn't mean teachers are powerless. Quite the opposite. While systemic change can be slow, change at the classroom level can be immediate. How teachers perceive, interact with, and treat their students can directly challenge deficit thinking. Furthermore, a single classroom can become a counterexample, serving as a balancing force against the negative reinforcement of the broader system. When enough classrooms make this shift, the systemic results begin to improve.

Research shows that lasting change doesn't emerge solely from top-down mandates but also through iterative, teacher-led shifts in practice (Bryk

---

16. Unlike us, who spent an embarrassing amount of time overanalyzing the problem of how to explain the anti-problem reaction to problems without sounding, well...anti-an-ti-problem. Sigh. Meta-traps are real.

et al., 2015; Fullan, 2011b). A culture of dignity can start in the classroom and, over time, scale upward (Cochran-Smith & Lytle, 2009; Senge, 1990).

Teaching with Dignity is both an act of resistance and an act of creation.

Teaching with Dignity: A Solution-Focused Approach

Dignity transcends being just another feel-good buzzword. It represents a concrete, robust solution to some of education's most enduring challenges, such as underperformance, disengagement, behavioral issues, and inequities. Instead of existing in a system that pushes you to react to problem after problem, imagine an environment designed to help teachers and students feel valued right from the start.

This shift isn't theoretical; it's practical and achievable. Schools that adopt human-centered theories and frameworks like Universal Design for Learning, Reggio Emilia, and Competency-Based Education move away from deficit-based thinking. They create environments where teachers, by default, view students as assets. These approaches consistently foster higher levels of student engagement, increased motivation, and more substantial long-term outcomes (Center for Applied Special Technology, 2018; Dweck, 2006; Edwards et al., 2012; Sturgis, 2017). (See Appendix E for a detailed list of frameworks.)

Education systems prioritizing dignity promote academic success, lower dropout rates, and enhance well-being (Organisation for Economic Co-operation and Development, 2024). Successful models such as Finland's student-centered approach, UNESCO's Learning Compass, and New Zealand's Te Whāriki focus on addressing students' needs rather than merely tackling challenges and perceived problems.

These approaches assume the innateness of dignity, and they know it needs to be honored for healthy growth. They model dignity as the solution to the core problem nestled within other education systems that do not serve students and teachers well. Before exploring practical strategies in subsequent chapters, it's crucial to understand the process of systems change.

The Balancing Loop of Dignity

Deficit thinking spirals into a self-perpetuating cycle (Figure 2.1). But just as harmful loops exist, so do positive counterforces. Figure 2.2 introduces a balancing loop, a stabilizing system that shifts education from reaction to creation. Teaching with dignity disrupts deficit thinking and restores equilibrium over time.

We've found that many people appreciate written explanations to accompany systems-thinking diagrams.[17] Here's a description of how teachers can break the harmful cycle fueled by deficit thinking through teaching with dignity.

1. **Shift Perspective:** View challenges through a lens of dignity rather than deficiency.

2. **Teach with Dignity:** Implement practices that honor student assets, such as their innate value and worth, experiences, strengths, personalities, and contributions.

3. **Belonging Improves:** A classroom culture of dignity fosters validation, connection, acceptance, and appreciation.

4. **Engagement Grows:** Students who feel they belong engage more consistently.

5. **Problems Decrease, Performance Increases:** Engagement fuels success, naturally diminishing problems.

↻ **Loop Continues:** As dignity becomes the norm, its seeds spread with every harvest, influencing the broader system.

---

17. This book was almost a wild ride through Systems Thinking, with diagrams at every turn and a tiny appendix titled *For Those Who Prefer Words*. But Floyd insists on actual sentences. Not too many, though. You're welcome.

FIGURE 2.2

Teaching with Dignity as a Balancing Loop

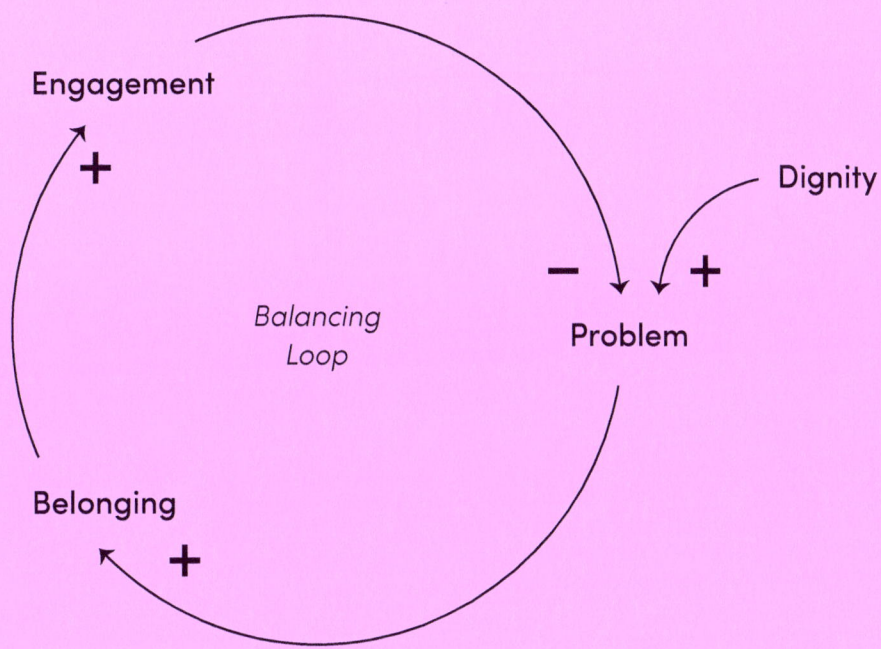

These steps, depicted by the balancing loop in Figure 2.2,[18] provide a balancing force for how individual teachers counter systemic deficit thinking. When done collectively, these steps shift the broader environment (school, district, etc.) from a culture in which reacting to problems is expected to one where undesirable outcomes naturally diminish because of the prevalence of dignity-centered behaviors, practices, and policies.

Shift Your Perspective

Breaking the cycle of harm starts with a shift in perspective: from seeing students as problems to seeing them as assets. That shift requires reexamining ingrained beliefs about learning and success.

---

18. People express love in different ways. Summer: acts of service. Floyd: blunt, direct feedback. John: Systems Thinking diagrams. If you ever receive one from him, just know he cares.

Mindsets shape everything. In *Think Again: The Power of Knowing What You Don't Know*, organizational psychologist and bestselling author Adam Grant (2021) argues that people tend to operate and keep operating within rigid, unexamined mental models that prevent them from improving. These mindsets can justify ineffective practices and policies, even when research suggests they don't work.

Grant (drawing on the work of decision-making expert Philip Tetlock) describes three typical mindsets or roles people take when defending their beliefs: preachers, prosecutors, or politicians. Take a look at Table 2.1 and see if you recognize these thinking styles in yourself, in your colleagues, or in school initiatives you've experienced.

TABLE 2.1

Common Mindsets in Thinking and Decision-Making

Mindset	Decisions and Actions	Limits
Preacher	Defends sacred beliefs and tries to convert others to their way of thinking.	Resistant to questioning assumptions. Focuses on what others need to change rather than on self-reflection.
Prosecutor	Focuses on proving others wrong and on attacking flawed arguments.	Prioritizes winning debates over seeking truth. Can shut down dialogue and new perspectives.
Politician	Seeks approval by campaigning for certain ideas or saying what is most popular.	Avoids difficult but necessary conversations. Lacks deep conviction or willingness to challenge norms.

Note: Summary of concepts based on Grant, 2021.

While these mindsets may seem like personal habits, they scale up to shape entire educational systems. They affect school culture, decision-making, and reform efforts. Think about times when these are true:

- **School improvement initiatives** become preaching sessions, where leaders insist on change but fail to model it themselves.

- **Professional development sessions** feel like courtroom battles, where presenters advocate for ideas while dismissing alternatives. This leaves teachers unconvinced and feeling blamed for systemic problems beyond their control.

- **Policy shifts** function as political maneuvers are introduced because they are popular or politically convenient, not because they work.

Within these scenarios, questioning the status quo is rare. Instead of examining whether an approach benefits students, individuals and organizations often double down, even when data may suggest they should move on and try something else. So, what's the alternative?[19] How can educators create real change if these mindsets keep schools stuck in outdated or ineffective approaches? Grant offers a fourth way, one that is both flexible and evidence driven: thinking like a scientist (Table 2.2).

---

19. Yes, we're aware that we're currently using a prosecutorial argument to convince you not to think like a prosecutor. Just go with it. We promise we're rethinking it...right after we finish making our case.

TABLE 2.2

Mindset Helpful for Growth and Decision Making

Thinking	Description	Effect	Requires
Scientist	Seeks truth by testing ideas and adapting to new findings.	Encourages reflection, innovation, and flexibility.	Curiosity, humility, and commitment to learning.

Note: Summary of concepts based on Grant, 2021.

Thinking like a scientist means valuing curiosity over certainty and humility over pride (Grant, 2021). Being open to seeking answers is what truly matters. While shifting to this mindset isn't easy, Grant explains it's easier when people build identity around values rather than around opinions and convictions. In other words, when teachers define their roles by honoring dignity (a value) instead of eliminating problems (a conviction), they cultivate the rich soil needed for student belonging, engagement, and achievement.

Rethinking your mindset means stepping away from sermons, battles, and political campaigns[20] and stepping toward curiosity, humility, and adaptability.

How to Think Like a Gardener

Green-thumb gardeners don't just plant seeds and hope for the best. They also observe, experiment, and adapt, much like scientists. A professional

---

20. Unless you're running for Teacher of the Year. If so, get Summer as your campaign manager. She's highly organized, insists on handling every detail, and somehow pulls off events that leave everyone speechless. Just be ready: Your acceptance speech will definitely come with a mandatory slide deck.

gardener is a specific kind of scientist called a horticulturist, applying scientific knowledge to cultivate healthy, flourishing environments. Educators can do the same.

Look at your classroom as if it were a garden.[21] Like plants, students grow at different rates and thrive under care, not control. The word "kindergarten" comes from the German *Kinder* (children) and *Garten* (garden), and is a reminder that teachers should cultivate learning, not force or factory-produce it.

It sounds simple enough, but simple isn't the same as easy.

- **Simple:** Every plant needs sunlight, water, air, and soil. In a garden, plants also need room for growth.
- **Hard:** Each plant requires different amounts of these resources. Some need shade, others full sun. Some prefer dry soil, while others thrive in constant moisture.
- **Hardest:** Tending to an entire ecosystem, ensuring every plant has what it needs while preventing overcrowding, nutrient depletion, or unhealthy competition.

A skilled gardener adapts to these challenges. They don't fix plants; they attend to essential resources to cultivate them. The same applies to teaching with dignity.

The Five Essential Resources for Teaching with Dignity

Just as a flourishing garden depends on the right conditions, so does a dignity-centered classroom. Each garden resource has a direct parallel with education.

---

21. Turns out Greg Lukianoff and Jonathan Haidt also recommend educators learn to think like gardeners in *The Coddling of the American Mind* (2018). Great minds mulch alike. We came to the metaphor through lived experience, but we're happy to share the compost.

Garden Resource	Classroom Equivalent	Purpose
Sunlight (vision)	Dignity Promise	A shared vision, co-created with students, that sets the aspirational goal for the community.
Water (trust)	Dignity Connectors	Meaningful, human-centered experiences that support social connectedness.
Air (ideas)	Dignity Expectations	Clear, co-created behavioral norms that sustain a positive learning environment.
Soil (actions)	Dignity Actions	The daily reality of the classroom culture: How students and teachers treat one another.
Room for Growth (improvement)	Dignity Ecosystem	A system that facilitates learning, adaptation, and evolution for teachers and students.

The remainder of this book unpacks these five essential resources, providing practical strategies for teaching with dignity. Keeping these essentials in focus allows every teacher to resist deficit thinking and build an ecosystem where students thrive.

What's Next?

Every garden begins with sunlight. It's what plants grow toward, and, in the light, we can see. Within our gardening analogy, we equate light with vision. Every dignity-centered classroom starts with a specific type of shared vision. We call it a Dignity Promise. This communal commitment is the sunlight that guides and energizes a learning community.

In the next chapter, we'll explore how to create a dignity-centered vision with your students. As sunlight makes growth possible, this vision sparks the culture that shapes everything ahead.

So grab your tools. The sun is rising. It's time to plant the first seed.

CHAPTER 3

Dignity Promise (Sunlight)

A new vision is needed, in which we see ourselves not as separate, but as part of a larger whole.

—Dalai Lama, 1999

The Sunrise of Dignity

Summer stood in front of her class, scanning the eager faces. Today, she and her students were taking their first step in creating a classroom culture based on dignity. For days, she'd led her second graders in exploring real-life examples of fairness and unfairness, and unconditional and conditional belonging.

They had seen and named what they didn't want: a classroom where kindness depended on cliques, some voices mattered more than others, and some students felt invisible while others took all the attention. Today, they would take the next step. They were ready to imagine and name exactly what they did want.

Summer took a steadying breath and smiled. "Close your eyes." The usual second-grade hum went quiet as students settled into the exercise.

"I want you to think about a time when you felt valued," Summer instructed, her voice soft. "When you felt like you truly mattered. Maybe it was when someone helped you or your ideas were listened to. Maybe it was when you felt safe, seen, or encouraged. Hold that feeling in your heart."

She let the silence linger, allowing space for reflection.

"Now, imagine that everyone in our classroom feels that way every day. Not just you, but every one of us. What would that look like? What would it sound like? What could we do to make that happen?"

Several students furrowed their brows in deep thought. Others sat completely still, eyes closed and faces softened with possibility.

Summer moved slowly through the room, watching their expressions. She drew heavily from Diane Maroney's *The Imagine Project* (2019) for this exercise. Maroney believed that imagination is primarily a gateway to hope, which is far more than just a creative exercise. Permit students to imagine beyond current limitations and they'll surprise you.

A small voice broke the silence. "We'd be kind to everyone."

Another chimed in, eyes snapping open. "We'd help each other when someone's having trouble."

"We'd clap when someone does something good!"

A quiet voice added, "The teacher would notice when we try our best."

Summer smiled. "Yes! And what about how we learn? How does our classroom feel when I'm teaching in a way that helps you feel important, valuable, and capable?"

The students paused. Then, a boy near the front spoke up. "We get to talk about what we think, not just answer questions."

"When you let us work together instead of always by ourselves," added Mia.

Jayden chimed in. "Or when you ask us what we want to learn about."

Excited murmurs spread around the room. Students continued to describe their aspirational learning environment, one where they all mattered. In doing so, they were doing more than just imagining how they would treat one another; they were envisioning a classroom where everything—including instruction—was designed to honor dignity.

Summer grabbed a marker and turned to the board. In bold letters, she wrote two words:

DIGNITY PROMISE

She turned back to the class, noticing the smiles. "We've been imagining what dignity looks like to us. That's our vision. I'll list our ideas about what we want our classroom to be. After that, we'll review the list, and then if we all agree, we'll commit as a group to making those things happen in our classroom. That's how we'll make our vision a reality. That's our Dignity Promise."

The students nodded. As Summer began listing their ideas, she knew this was more than just a classroom activity. This was also hope made visible and the beginning of something bigger. They would make it a beacon, a guiding light to call them back to safety again and again. This would be their vision, their commitment, and an illumination that would shape their path forward.

Imagination as Spark, Vision as Light

As you can see, we began this chapter with another real-life scene from Summer's classroom. A picture can paint a thousand words, and Summer's story brings our theories to life. Dignity begins with imagination, seeing beyond the limitations of what's possible. Summer led her students in an exercise in hope, which meant something better was possible; the class could co-create a place where they could thrive.

Trauma expert Diane Maroney (2019) describes imagination as the spark that bypasses doubt and fear,[22] allowing people to see beyond barriers. Einstein went so far as to claim, "Imagination is more important than knowledge." Research backs this: Future-focused thinking makes people more likely to take steps toward that future (Destin & Oyserman, 2010). This is why Summer's activity was electrifying. Imagining what was possible sparked the students' motivation to commit to what they imagined.

But imagination isn't enough. After all, a spark must catch flame before it provides the light needed for a task. In dignity teaching, light is the shared vision, the sustaining force that helps turn possibility into reality. Even the best ideas remain untethered without a clear vision, leading to reactive actions and unfocused progress.

Stephen Covey (1989) called a clear vision "Beginning with the End in Mind,"[23] just as Summer did with her students so they knew what they

---

22. In retrospect, our elementary teachers probably could have helped us bypass the fear of imminent doom from quicksand, acid rain, and the Bermuda Triangle. Turns out, those threats weren't exactly on par with nuclear war: Quicksand wasn't lurking in every suburban backyard, planes and ships weren't vanishing daily in the Bermuda Triangle, and acid rain wasn't about to melt our faces like *Raiders of the Lost Ark*. We probably should have been encouraged to imagine seatbelts and sunscreen.

23. Overused? Trite? Absolutely. We tried to leave it to bumper stickers and over-laminated posters. But as it turns out, Covey was right. Beginning with the end in mind works.

would be working toward. Thus, the Dignity Promise represents a goal, aspiration, or intention. It bridges imagination and action, enabling people to transform abstract values into real-world, concrete success criteria.[24] (More on this in Chapter Five.)

This isn't just a nice-sounding theory. When students co-create a collective vision, they also develop a stronger sense of ownership, leading to greater motivation, engagement, and accountability (Ryan & Deci, 2000; Zimmerman, 2002). Instead of passively receiving imposed policies and just following the rules, they see themselves as active participants in shaping their learning environment (Cook-Sather, 2006).

A Dignity Promise is a commitment to uphold dignity in daily interactions. But for it to work, it must be lived, not just declared.

Co-Creation and Commitment

This type of shared vision holds the potential to guide the class, school, or community toward a better version of itself. It's neither a rigid set of rules nor a top-down mandate; co-creation is essential. Research on autonomy and motivation (Deci & Ryan, 2000) shows that people are more likely to uphold agreements they helped create. That's why students take ownership of the Dignity Promise and assume responsibility for turning it into action when they have a voice in shaping it.

A co-created vision fosters the following:

- **Autonomy:** Students feel empowered when their voices shape their vision.

_____

24. In *Back to the Future*, Marty McFly learned that *The Power of Love* (abstraction) was more than a Huey Lewis banger; it was the solution to the real-world problem with his timeline. Likewise, a Dignity Promise isn't just words on a poster. It takes significant commitment (perhaps 1.21 gigawatts' worth) to turn words into daily actions. No DeLorean or flux capacitor needed.

- **Accountability:** They uphold the values they help create rather than following imposed rules.
- **Commitment:** They are more personally invested in making expectations a reality when self-determined.

Once created, a Dignity Promise must be acted on. If it's just words written and then forgotten, it becomes meaningless. To ensure it stays alive and meaningful, teachers must make the Dignity Promise:

☑ **Co-created:** Shaped with students, making it personal and meaningful.

☑ **Visible:** Displayed in the classroom, referenced in discussions, and reinforced in daily interactions.

☑ **Revisited:** Used as a guidepost for classroom culture, especially during challenges.

A simple class-wide Dignity Promise might sound like this: "In this classroom, everyone belongs. We treat each other as equals, celebrate each other's successes, and ensure no one is left behind."

The process works at a larger scale, too. Schools and districts can guide students, staff, and families to create a broader pledge, uniting the community under shared values that uphold human value and worth. Coincidentally, a Dignity Pledge is how Donna Hicks (2018) describes the process of formalizing shared values into a commitment to honor dignity in every interaction. Some call it a Promise, others a Pledge, but the name isn't what matters.

What matters is that the Pledge or Promise leads to meaningful action. Without that, even the best intentions risk becoming little more than words on a wall. The community needs to practice its Dignity Promise, reinforcing and weaving it into daily interactions; they must live it, not just proclaim it.

Beyond the Posters and Platitudes

Too often, well-intended efforts fall into the trap of symbolism over substance. Schools may proclaim values like inclusion and belonging, but if students' daily experiences contradict those ideals, the words become empty gestures at best.

In his *Education Week* opinion piece "Stop Telling Students, 'You Belong,'" social psychologist Gregory Walton (2021) cautions that performative gestures such as posters, slogans, and school marquee messages can backfire if they lack meaningful action to support them.[25] A school that simply declares, "You belong!" without creating genuine conditions for belonging and seeking evidence that students are experiencing belonging risks adding insult to injury. Students, especially those struggling to feel like they matter, can sense when a promise is empty. This disconnect between words and reality is why dignity must be an active practice, and not a passive declaration.

That's why a Dignity Promise is a culture-building tool, not a compliance tool. It reminds communities that they must practice dignity, and not just proclaim it. Imagining and defining dignity can't end with a poster on a wall. A Dignity Promise is meaningful only when it shapes daily interactions.

To be effective, a community must practice its Dignity Promise:

- **Students** don't just follow rules; they also shape and uphold their classroom's values.
- **Teachers** don't just enforce policies; they also model the Promise and nurture an environment where dignity is a daily reality.
- **Schools** don't just discuss inclusion and belonging; they also make them real.

---

25. Sort of like when we, as 13-year-olds, thought swapping in neon-colored laces on high-tops would make us the epitome of cool. Turns out, it takes more than flashy messages to make something real.

When students and teachers live the Promise, action occurs at every level: individual, classroom, and schoolwide (if not even broader). Dignity isn't a slogan. It's a shared responsibility.[26]

How to Create a Dignity Promise

Here's a step-by-step guide to creating a Dignity Promise that moves beyond words into meaningful action.

1. **Imagine the Ideal State:** Visualize a community where dignity is honored, and people feel they matter. What actions do you see? What is happening?

2. **Brainstorm Descriptors:** Identify the values, actions, and aspirations that define a culture of dignity.

3. **Synthesize and Seek Consensus:** Refine and combine descriptors into concise, shared statements that reflect the community's vision.

4. **Commit to the Promise:** Display, reference, and reinforce the Promise in daily practice to ensure its relevance.

Figure 3.1 offers examples of a Dignity Promise across different contexts: elementary classrooms, schools, secondary schools, and district offices. While these examples may involve written statements or displayed pledges, the true purpose extends beyond words. A Dignity Promise is more than a declaration; it also serves as the foundation for ensuring that every interaction, decision, and policy upholds the fundamental belief that dignity is a right to be honored, not a privilege to be earned.

---

26. This is much like assembling a full *Voltron*, the giant robot made of five mechanical lions that ruled the 1985 afterschool television lineup. If one lion is missing, you're not saving the galaxy—you're just four awkward robot cats with attitude.

FIGURE 3.1

Dignity Promise Examples

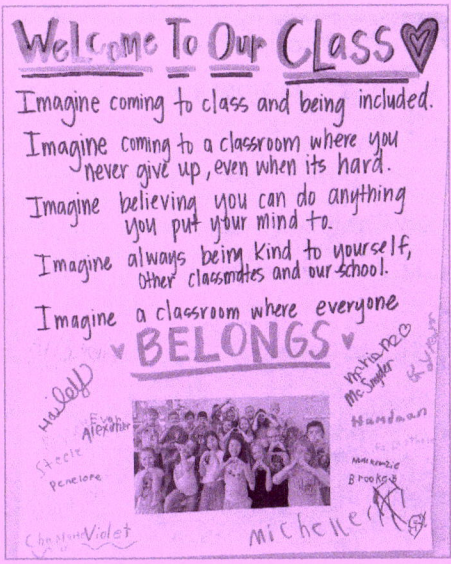

Welcome To Our Class ♥

Imagine coming to class and being included.

Imagine coming to a classroom where you never give up, even when its hard.

Imagine believing you can do anything you put your mind to.

Imagine always being kind to yourself, other classmates and our school!

Imagine a classroom where everyone ♥ BELONGS ♥

WOODLAND ELEMENTARY JUST CAUSE

Imagine feeling a sense of belonging where you are valued, seen, and heard.

Imagine taking action in equity, celebrating diversity and empowering others.

Imagine believing all children can learn.

Imagine engaging in an inclusive, dynamic, and resilient culture.

Imagine creating a brave space that sparks joy, wonder and a passion for learning.

Be **Bold**. Be **Brave**. Be **Brilliant**. Be a **Bear**.

Dreams to Reality—

- Imagine a school with a supportive positive flexible vibe that allows for (S) driven laughter and discussion.
- Imagine a school with no judgement, open communication, cohesiveness, inclusion and a safe place to be who you are ⟨ students staff families community
- Imagine a school with plentiful collaboration, calmness, and thoughtful empathetic people supporting one another ♥

---

* Imagine a place where I am free to be me, where trust and collaboration thrive, and no one tells me what to do.

* Imagine a place where I have the tools I need, the space to create, and a learning environment that inspires growth and discovery.

* Imagine a place where competency is celebrated, responsibility is embraced, autonomy is nurtured, and professionals are given the space and time to grow, thrive, and excel.

* Imagine a place where time is optimized, stress minimized, trusted systems guide your work, and established processes ensure focus, efficiency, and meaningful opportunities without unnecessary effort.

* Imagine a place where building strong relationships is at the heart of everything, lunch breaks are a time to connect, snacks are shared, and a sense of community is fostered.

Note: Moving clockwise starting in the upper left corner: elementary classroom, elementary school staff, district office staff, middle school team.

Case Study: The Mesquite Promise

A Dignity Promise can shape communities much larger than a classroom. In early 2021, Mesquite Independent School District in Texas set out to do just that after identifying their challenge: How could they move beyond compliance-based training to build a culture of dignity that extended beyond schools and into the entire city?

Seeking a more sustainable approach, they partnered with us (John and Floyd) to embed dignity into its districtwide mission. Dr. LaDonna Gulley initially reached out, frustrated by the ineffectiveness of one-off anti-bias training. Like many leaders, she saw little long-term, positive change from these efforts (Kalev et al., 2006; Paluk et al., 2021; Sparks, 2020). Instead, she sought a more-enduring solution that fostered communitywide commitment rather than temporary compliance.

LaDonna led a community-driven effort to create a shared vision for nearly a year. She led a broad coalition of stakeholders, including the following:

- **Public institutions:** City leaders, school district leaders, and local organizations
- **Neighborhood groups:** Homeowners' associations, youth sports coaches, and parent and family networks
- **Students and educators:** Teachers, administrators, and students themselves

Through this collaborative process, they co-created The Mesquite Promise, a shared commitment to honoring dignity across schools and the entire community (Figure 3.2). Businesses displayed the Promise in their windows, the mayor referenced it in speeches, and highway billboards spread the message citywide. The impact? Increased trust, accountability, and engagement throughout the community; it was a cultural shift.

FIGURE 3.2

The Mesquite Promise

THE MESQUITE PROMISE

You were made to excel.
take initiative
be accountable
set ambitious goals
pursue your passion

You belong here.
be authentic
seek new experiences
invest in relationships
open your mind

Your dignity is a given.
own your worth
value every human
stop and think
give grace

You are a difference maker.
have radical empathy
never give up
speak life
be bold

#YouBelongInMesquite

Note: Reproduced in black and white with permission from Mesquite Independent School District.

This model offers a scalable alternative to Summer's single-classroom approach, particularly for secondary teachers who teach multiple daily classes. Rather than creating separate Dignity Promises for each class, schools can develop department-wide, grade-level, or schoolwide versions to ensure consistency while still honoring student voices.

As you can see, the Dignity Promise works at any scale. Whether it's a single classroom or an entire city, the essential process remains the same:

- **Dream it.** Imagine a classroom, school, or community where people feel valued.
- **Define it.** Collaboratively articulate the aspirational values and goals to bring this vision to life.
- **Live it.** Make dignity an everyday practice, a lived reality in policy, culture, instruction, and relationships, and not just an ideal.

Mesquite's success proves that a collective commitment to dignity is possible and scalable.

From Imagination to Action: Sustaining a Culture of Dignity

Although co-creating a Dignity Promise begins with defining values, it doesn't end there. The goal is to put these defined values into practice in everyday life.

As Summer's students demonstrated, a shared vision reshapes culture. When students take ownership of dignity, they carry it beyond the classroom, influencing how they interact in hallways, playgrounds, and even outside school.

On a larger scale, The Mesquite Promise showed how this ripple effect can transform an entire city. When a group unites under a shared vision of dignity, it fosters collective responsibility, making ideals like fairness and belonging become lived realities rather than abstract concepts.

Regardless of scale, a Dignity Promise serves as the core of transformation so that people can more easily make their communities places that bring out the best in each individual. The idea that the light of a shared vision is the source of growth and improvement isn't an arbitrary belief; various religious, philosophical, and cultural traditions view light as creation's first and most essential element. It's the force that illuminates, sustains life, and guides.[27] Similarly, a Dignity Promise is the light in our classrooms and communities. It's the primary resource that nurtures and empowers everything else.

------

27. Much like *E.T. the Extra-Terrestrial*, pointing that glowing finger, we all need a little guiding light. (Although Floyd is still working through the childhood trauma of seeing E.T. go home.)

But vision alone isn't enough. Just as plants need more than sunlight to survive and thrive, classrooms require additional resources to flourish. Our next step is to examine the essential resource of water.

If sunlight (vision) directs a classroom community, then water (connection) ensures the community is nurtured and supported. Water represents positive social connectedness: the trust, mutual regard, and belonging that allows people to experience dignity, not just imagine it. Even the best vision (and the strongest plant) withers without water.

Dignity Connectors keep the classroom culture thriving. Like water enabling plants to absorb and engage with nutrients, Dignity Connectors facilitate social and academic engagement, helping students and teachers recognize their connection to dignity within themselves, with others, and the classroom community.

We focus the next chapter on water and connection. Stay with us; this is just the beginning of teaching with dignity.

Let's keep growing.

CHAPTER 4

Dignity Connectors (Water)

When we know ourselves to be connected to all others, acting compassionately is simply the natural thing to do.

—Rachel Naomi Remen, 2000

The Flow of Summer's Morning Meeting

Summer knew her students enjoyed their daily Morning Meetings and especially looked forward to Fridays. Each week ended with gratitude-focused reflections, where students talked about how they and their classmates had upheld the Dignity Promise during the past week.

The classroom hummed with anticipation. On an easel, Summer placed a colorful poster displaying that morning's discussion prompts. The early January sunlight streamed through the windows, casting long streaks across the rug where twenty-three second graders sat cross-legged. Summer took a deep breath, her voice calm and inviting.

"Good morning, everyone." She let the words sink in and then continued. "Before we start, let's take a deep breath together." She inhaled deeply, and the students followed, their quiet focus settling over the room.

"How has everyone been doing with keeping our Dignity Promise this week?" she asked. "I'll go first. Yesterday at recess, I noticed several of you inviting others to join your games. You made sure no one felt left out. Thank you for keeping our Promise so well."

She held up a small jar filled with folded slips of paper. "Today, we're making our gratitude sharing extra special. Each of you will pull a name and then share something that person has done this week to uphold our Dignity Promise."

She handed the jar to Jayden, who unwrapped a slip and studied the name. Usually reserved, Jayden had started participating more, and Summer wanted to encourage that. His voice was quiet but steady.

"I'm grateful for Mia because she helped me with my math yesterday."

Mia beamed, and a chorus of "Good job, Mia!" rippled through the circle. Summer smiled, letting the moment linger and be savored.

"That was a wonderful way to start us off, Jayden. Thank you for sharing."

The circle continued, students drawing names and offering heartfelt gratitude. "I'm grateful for Ethan because he helped me organize the books on the shelf." Then, "Ava made sure I wasn't sitting alone during snack time."

Summer occasionally added her observations, ensuring everyone felt seen and valued. "I noticed Sandy taking time to explain her project to a friend who was struggling," she said. Sandy's face lit up.

As each child spoke, Summer could see their confidence grow. These weren't just routine reflections. The students were shaping their classroom culture by recognizing and reinforcing belonging, kindness, and dignity in everyday actions.

She planned for this conversation to extend beyond the circle time. When the gratitude round finished, she announced, "Later, during English Language Arts, we'll take our gratitude a step further. You'll each write a thank-you letter to a classmate, letting them know how their actions made a difference."

Summer turned to the blackboard and wrote two words in large letters: DIGNITY and RESPECT. She looked around the room and began, "You know, people sometimes mix up dignity and respect, and today, I'd like to point out the difference because it's important.[28] Dignity is something we all have because we're human. It's a word that describes the innate worth we were born with. Respect, on the other hand, is an attitude people can have about you. Respect can be earned or lost based on our actions."

She paused to let that sink in. "Our Dignity Promise reminds us that we treat everyone as valuable, even if we don't always agree with them, like them, or admire what they do. Treating people poorly violates our own dignity as much as it hurts the other person's."

A few students nodded thoughtfully.

"Think about ways we can honor someone's dignity, even when we don't agree or are upset with them," she continued. "Remember that honoring dignity isn't the same as being nice or trying to make people feel happy all the time. Sometimes, it means not being cruel, humiliating, or harm-

---

28. When we learned this from Donna Hicks, it felt like learning Darth Vader's identity for the first time. "I am your father," resulted in blown minds, silent theaters, and existential crises among kids everywhere in 1980 and 1981.

ing others. Close your eyes if it helps you focus. When you're ready, raise your hand."

Mia was the first to respond. "Honoring dignity means listening to someone when they're talking, even if you don't agree with what they're saying."

Summer nodded. "Yes! Listening shows that we acknowledge them and that their ideas are worth understanding, even if we don't see eye-to-eye."

Ethan added, "It means not laughing at someone when they make a mistake."

"Oh, yes," Summer agreed. "Mistakes are how we learn. Being laughed at feels humiliating. Instead, we can help them feel safe enough to keep trying."

The conversation wove through more moments of insight and connection. One student shared an experience of feeling excluded at recess, and another immediately offered a solution: "You can play with me next time."

Summer relished the culture they were building together. As the meeting drew to a close, she reflected aloud. "What I love about this class is how you honor dignity daily. You listen to each other, help one another, and make sure no one feels left out.

"That's what it means to honor dignity—showing people they matter. That's not always easy, especially when we disagree or lose respect for someone. But you all rise to the challenge, and I couldn't be prouder. You are the most awesome class I've ever had."

A ripple of smiles and excited murmurs spread through the circle. "You're the awesomest teacher!" someone called out, and a few students clapped.

Summer laughed, shaking her head. "Alright, alright, let's not get carried away," she teased. "But seriously, you all make this classroom a special place."

The students grinned, happy and secure in the culture they were building together.

Dignity Connectors Meet a Fundamental Need

We can all feel happy as we read how splendidly well teaching with dignity worked in Summer's classroom. Remember, these were the dark days after COVID-19. Not much was working splendidly within schools.

Summer's students demonstrated warmth, trust, and mutual respect during the Morning Meeting, and that positive flow wasn't accidental. It was the direct result of structures designed to help students feel connected. We call these structures Dignity Connectors, and they keep a classroom culture thriving.

Humans need to connect with others, and these interactions should honor our dignity. A Dignity Connector is any intentional routine, activity, or structure that fosters healthy connections within the classroom. Think of a Connector as a pipe.[29] The pipe carries the water of positive social connectedness (rapport, trust, mutual support, etc.), ensuring that relationships aren't just planted and forgotten, but instead are nurtured and fed continuously.

---

29. Not to be confused with the pipes in *Super Mario Bros.*, which mostly led to underground trouble or an alarming number of fire-breathing plants. Our Dignity Connector pipes actually take you somewhere good.

Let's use our gardening analogy for context to better understand Dignity Connectors. While sunlight provides direction for growth, plants can't survive on sunlight alone. They need water. If the Dignity Promise provides sunlight within the classroom ecosystem, Dignity Connectors carry and deliver the water. They are the daily actions and structures that transport the nutrients of dignity to the plants to sustain growth and keep relationships thriving.

Then there's our water metaphor.[30] Think of it this way: if Social Connection is the need, then Social Connectedness is the extent to which that need is met. Positive Social Connectedness is when that need is met in a way that enhances well-being and dignity; it's the clean, nourishing water that allows people to thrive. And Dignity Connectors? They are the structures that enable hydration: the channels, pipelines, and reservoirs that ensure this wholesome water reaches every student in the classroom (see Table 4.1).

These Connectors facilitate the flow that strengthens relationships, helping students engage meaningfully with themselves, their teachers, and their classmates. When Dignity Connectors are in place, students do more than sit in the same room and coexist; they also develop meaningful relationships and a stronger sense of community.

Dignity Connectors work by doing the following:

- **Creating opportunities for social connectedness**, ensuring that relationships have the conditions to grow and belonging has space to take hold.

- **Providing pathways for engagement** so students don't just feel included, but also actively participate in a supportive

---

30. This is dangerously close to the ecosystem poster our fifth-grade science teachers had right next to the "Hang in There" kitten. But stick with us; this one won't be on a multiple-choice test.

TABLE 4.1

Key Terms Related to Dignity Connectors

Term	Role	Definition
Social Connection	Need	The fundamental **human need** to build and maintain meaningful relationships with others, characterized by feelings of closeness, care, and being valued.
Social Connectedness	Fulfillment	The **degree of fulfillment of the need** for relationships, ranging from isolation to deep interpersonal engagement, as experienced by an individual or group.
Positive Social Connectedness	Ideal State	A **healthy state of fulfilling the need** for relationships in a way that is enriching and supportive, and that contributes to well-being and a sense of belonging.
Dignity Connector	Sustaining Mechanism	A **practice, activity, or structure** that strengthens positive social connectedness by reinforcing a sense of worth in oneself and others, fostering mutual regard, and supporting a community's well-being and shared purpose.

learning environment.

- ☑ **Reinforcing dignity through interaction** allows students to see their value and worth reflected in how they are treated and how they treat others.

When educators intentionally integrate Dignity Connectors into their classrooms' daily routines, they equip students with the skills to build mutual respect, trust, and belonging that will extend far beyond the classroom walls.

The Heart of a Dignity-Centered Classroom

The structures that sustain dignity in a classroom don't operate in the background; they are woven into every interaction, guiding how students engage with one another. More than occasional activities, Dignity Connectors form the dependable relational pathways or pipelines that run in a grid across the garden and ensure no student is left on the margins.

Dignity Connectors are intentional. They don't happen by chance any more than the watering grid in a garden magically appears. While casual moments of impromptu interaction can and do spark relationships, sustaining positive community connectedness requires intentional design. Dignity Connectors do this by providing an ongoing structure for three essential elements of classroom relationships:

- ☑ **Trust:** Establishing a sense of security in relationships.
- ☑ **Collaboration:** Creating opportunities to work together meaningfully.
- ☑ **Effective Communication:** Encouraging active listening and dialogue.

Let's look at Summer's Morning Meetings again. More than just a warm-up activity, they created a predictable, structured space where students practice relational skills:

- **Active listening** → Showing that every voice matters.
- **Empathy** → Understanding and validating others' experiences.
- **Mutual care** → Strengthening bonds and reinforcing dignity.

Morning meetings are just one example of an effective connection-building structure. In other classrooms committed to dignity, restorative circles give students a framework to navigate conflict. Peer mentorship programs build ongoing opportunities for connection and support. These are Dignity Connectors, structures that help positive social connectedness become the norm in a classroom.

When positive social connectedness defines classroom culture, students feel safe, engaged, and ready to thrive.[31] Far better than merely showing up for class, students are safer when they build relationships based on trust and consistency, are more engaged when they feel connected to their peers and the learning community, and are equipped to thrive when they know they are valued contributors to the classroom.

A dignity-centered classroom integrates social connection with academic instruction. It's a place where students experience learning as a shared human endeavor because connection is the foundation for positive classroom activity.

Connection Before Content

To some educators, cultivating meaningful connectedness may seem like it's above and beyond delivering content. Maybe so. Yet it's also es-

---

31. Much like how we felt as fifth-graders who finally got our hands on an official Trapper Keeper: safe, organized, and undeniably cooler than when we had the plain old three-ring binders.

sential. Before students can fully engage with academic material, they must feel safe, valued, and connected to their peers, teachers, and the classroom experience.

More than a nice idea or an extra luxury, connection helps students learn. Research consistently shows that, when students experience strong social connectedness, their academic and personal outcomes improve. They participate more actively, take more significant risks in their learning, and develop the resilience to persist through challenges (American Psychological Association [APA], 2023; Walton & Cohen, 2011).

Teachers can use Dignity Connectors to operationalize this principle and embed uplifting relationships into the classroom. Rather than treating human connection as an occasional add-on or an isolated episode, dignity-centered teachers build connections throughout the learning process because they know it matters (MIT Teaching & Learning Lab, n.d.). Table 4.2 highlights the far-reaching effects of positive social connectedness in student development.

The use of Dignity Connectors can facilitate these positive outcomes. Even a quick activity at the start of a lesson (sometimes called icebreakers) can encourage students to get to know each other better and provide opportunities to develop positive social connectedness.

The Power and Pitfalls of Icebreakers

When done well, the benefits of icebreakers far outweigh the risks. Research shows that structured icebreakers improve engagement and reduce hesitancy, setting the stage for meaningful participation (Kilanowski, 2012). Pamela Cantor, M.D., an expert in the science of learning and development, explains, "The driver for learning is the social connection. Activating a child's cognitive skills begins with activating their social

TABLE 4.2

Effects of Positive Social Connectedness

Outcome	Students Experiencing Positive Social Connectedness are...
Engagement in Learning	More likely to participate in class, show curiosity, and invest effort in their education.
Academic Success	More likely to have stronger overall academic performance, better grades, and improved test scores.
Healthy Behaviors	More likely to follow school rules and less likely to engage in risky behaviors like substance abuse or absenteeism.
Social Skills	More likely to form healthy relationships and display emotional regulation, effective communication, and empathy.
Sense of Belonging	More able to develop stronger identification within the classroom, fostering commitment and engagement.
Mental Health and Well-Being	More likely to have overall well-being; and less likely to experience depression, stress, and anxiety.
Resourcefulness	More likely to reach out to teachers, peers, or counselors for academic or personal assistance when facing difficulties.
Resilience	Better equipped to handle setbacks and persist in adversity.

Note: Summary of table content adapted from J. Allen et al. (2008), R. Blum et al. (2002), Collaborative for Academic, Social, and Emotional Learning (2020), and M. Gopalan & S. Brady (2019).

connectedness." (Edutopia, 2019, 0:01) This is because psychological safety—the feeling of security in a learning space—plays a crucial role in students' ability to process and retain information.

However, educators often misuse icebreakers, treating them as a throw-away activity or an obligatory start to a training session, meeting, or class.[32] We've all been there. Surely, you can recall a staff meeting or professional development session where the icebreaker felt disconnected. The facilitator moved on as if it had never happened or even said, "Now, let's get started." The implication? The activity wasn't essential and had nothing to do with the actual work. At best, it was a waste of time; at worst, an insult to people's intelligence.

This misuse sends the wrong message, obviously. When educators treat icebreakers as formalities rather than foundational, students and work-shop participants disengage. The real power of an icebreaker is not the activity itself but how it's connected to the learning process. When used skillfully, an icebreaker is an on-ramp to meaningful participation and learning, not just a trite warm-up. A good icebreaker helps every student build trust, have fun, and receive the message: "This classroom is a place where you belong, and your voice matters."

Make Connection Part of Learning

Although icebreakers can enrich the learning process, they aren't enough by themselves. The most effective teachers do more than establish connections at the beginning of a lesson; they also weave connections into the entire learning process and broader learning environment.

---

32. Yes, we've all suffered through these. They're the professional equivalent of forced family fun, like being dragged to the mall, in the back of the station wagon, for a RadioShack grand opening or a family portrait session in matching sweaters. At least we could get an Orange Julius, though. Right?!

Even small moments, such as partner discussions during a lesson, can have a lasting impact (Ma et al., 2022). These moments reinforce that connection isn't a preliminary step before the real work begins; it is part of the actual work. When a teacher prompts students to discuss a question with a peer, students experience more than an exchange of information. They're strengthening relational confidence. A thoughtfully structured peer collaboration activity can build trust, ease tension, and encourage deeper engagement with the material during lessons (APA, 2023).

But before lessons even begin, connection strategies such as Positive Greetings at the Door help to maximize academic engagement (Cook, Fiat, et al., 2018). In classrooms where teachers consistently used the Positive Greetings at the Door protocol, student engagement increased by over 20%, while disciplinary referrals dropped by nearly 10%.[33] One might minimize this strategy as a polite gesture, but it's much more. It's akin to watering the soil, which is a high-impact, low-cost gardening strategy. By nurturing a sense of belonging when students arrive, teachers create the conditions for engagement to take root and grow throughout the day's lessons.

No matter when or how they happen in the classroom, moments of connection prime the brain for learning by lowering anxiety and activating social motivation, which is the drive to participate, contribute, and persist (MIT Teaching & Learning Lab, n.d.). Thus, teaching with dignity recognizes these facts:

☑ Connection is essential, not extra.

☑ A sense of belonging is a prerequisite for deep learning, not an add-on.

---

33. Numbers like these would have had ten-year old Floyd reaching for his Casio calculator watch and a Tony Gwynn stat sheet. After all, if teachers were measured like Gwynn at the plate, anyone consistently boosting engagement by 20% would be a first-ballot inductee into the Teacher Hall of Fame.

☑ Dignity-honoring actions are woven into the fabric of the classroom and how lessons unfold, not just during interpersonal dynamics.

Since you've chosen to read this book, you're likely already aware that the more teachers integrate connection with content, the more they build classrooms where students move beyond simply trying to absorb information to engaging, growing, and thriving. Even if this isn't news to you, we've found it helpful to name specific Dignity Connector structures. Table 4.3 offers several examples of research-backed practices.

TABLE 4.3

Examples of Dignity Connectors

Practice	Research Citations
Effective Icebreakers	Kilanowski, J. F. (2012). Breaking the ice: A pre-intervention strategy to engage research participants. *Journal of Pediatric Health Care, 26(3)*, 209–212.
Positive Greetings at the Door	Cook, C. R., Fiat, A., Larson, M., Daikos, C., Slemrod, T., Holland, E. A., Thayer, A. J., & Renshaw, T. (2018). Positive greetings at the door: Evaluation of a low-cost, high-yield proactive classroom management strategy. *Journal of Positive Behavior Interventions, 20(3)*, 149–159.
Effective Group Work	Cohen, E. G. (1994). *Designing group work: Strategies for the heterogeneous classroom* (2nd ed.). Teachers College Press.
Cooperative Learning Structures	Johnson, D. W., Johnson, R. T., & Holubec, E. J. (1994). *Cooperation in the classroom* (6th ed.). Interaction Book Company. Kagan, S., & Kagan, L. (2009). *Kagan cooperative learning*. Kagan Publishing.

Discussion Protocols	McDonald, J. P., Mohr, N., Dichter, A., & McDonald, E. C. (2013). *The power of protocols: An educator's guide to better practice* (3rd ed.). Teachers College Press.
Active Listening	Rogers, C. R., & Farson, R. E. (1957). *Active listening.* Industrial Relations Center, University of Chicago.
Welcoming Rituals	Collaborative for Academic, Social, and Emotional Learning (CASEL). (2020). *SEL 3 signature practices playbook: A toolkit for educators.* https://casel.org
Restorative Circles	Evans, K., & Vaandering, D. (2012). *The little book of restorative justice in education: Fostering responsibility, healing, and hope in schools.* Good Books.
Brain Breaks	Mahar, M. T. (2011). Impact of short bouts of physical activity on attention-to-task in elementary school children. *Preventive Medicine, 52,*S60–S64. https://doi.org/10.1016/j.ypmed.2011.01.026

Sustaining the Flow of Dignity

Dignity Connectors provide the relational water that nourishes classroom culture, and sustaining this flow requires consistent care and reflection. After all, a gardener doesn't simply water her plants once and walk away, so teachers must continuously assess the effectiveness of their Dignity Connectors and adjust them to meet their students' evolving needs.

In Summer's classroom, Morning Meetings weren't just routines but also lifelines of connection, sustaining a dignity-centered culture. Through intentional practices like gratitude shares and facilitated group discussions, Summer ensured that dignity was something her students could see, feel, and live. These Dignity Connectors acted as water, nourishing relationships and creating an environment where every student felt valued, worthy, and capable of growth.

As important as all of this is, we offer this caveat: Teachers have a responsibility to balance relationships with academic standards. Remember, even the most well-intentioned practices can have unintended consequences if not appropriately balanced. In gardening, overwatering can lead to root rot,[34] weakening the plant rather than strengthening it. Similarly, an excessive focus on relationships at the expense of academic rigor can undermine student achievement. Research indicates that, while strong teacher-student relationships are essential, they work in tandem with high academic expectations to foster social and educational growth (Bryk et al., 2010).

When connection and content enrich one another, they cultivate mutual care and belonging, which fosters academic success. In other words, students experience the conditions that help them flourish socially and academically. Even though some critics might say they don't have time for relationships in the classroom, the truth is that they don't have time not to tend to them. Dignity Connectors support academic achievement through healthy relationships. Research proves that relational attributes such as empathy and warmth improve academic performance directly, as well as indirectly, by increasing students' sense of belonging (Cai et al., 2023; Cornelius-White, 2007).

Your Next Step

So far, we've explored the role of the Dignity Promise (sunlight) and Dignity Connectors (water) in cultivating a classroom where every student can thrive. But plants also need air. Plants take in carbon dioxide to grow, and their roots seek oxygen in the spaces between the soil particles. This makes air the third essential resource.

---

34. Unintended consequences: the backbone of 1980s decision-making. *New Coke* made everyone hoard the original formula, Atari rushed a glitchy *Pac-Man* game and had to bury tons of unsold cartridges in a New Mexico landfill, and "computer class" in school (aka playing *Lemonade Stand* and *The Oregon Trail*) left us with elite supply-chain strategies and wagon-fording instincts, but questionable typing skills.

Just as air sustains life in a garden, clear behavioral expectations sustain dignity in a classroom. We call these Dignity Expectations, and teachers and students co-create and use them to shape an environment where dignity shifts from aspiration to action.

You're doing great! So far, you've learned how to ensure proper sunlight and water flow. In the next chapter, we'll explore how Dignity Expectations function like air, providing the structure that reinforces and strengthens dignity-honoring actions.

Take a breath. It's almost time to aerate the soil.

CHAPTER 5

Dignity Expectations (Air)

You can't be what you can't see.

—Marian Wright Edelman, 1992

The Clean Air of Clear Expectations

"Okay, team," Summer announced, standing by the whiteboard, marker in hand. She scanned the circle of second graders on the rug. Each student sat beside a discussion partner. Students move from partner to the next, so by the end of the marking period, every student would have worked every other student at least once.

"Yesterday, we chose four dignity components for our classroom. We named acceptance and acknowledgment. What were the other two?"

"Recognition and inclusion!" several voices chorused.

"Exactly!" Summer smiled. "Today, we'll take those four ideas and create something special: a Code of Collaboration." She paused. "With your partner, take 30 seconds to discuss: What does collaboration mean?"

After a brief buzz of conversation, she rang her chime, the familiar cue for students to wind down and refocus on her.

"Collaboration is working together," Summer said. "Our Code of Collaboration will show how we work together in our classroom to live out our Dignity Promise daily. And if we want our Code of Collaboration to work, we need to get clear on what these dignity components look and sound like so we know when we're doing them well."

She turned to the board, where the word "Recognition" was written and underlined, with space underneath.

"Let's start with recognition. How do we show it? How do we let others know we see and appreciate their efforts?"

She let the silence sit for a few seconds. "Now, turn to your partner and share ideas."

Pairs leaned in, voices bubbling with ideas. Summer waited, catching snippets of conversation now and then. After a few minutes, she rang her chime.

"Let's hear some of your awesome ideas."

Ava's hand shot up. "You can say, 'Good job!' when someone works hard."

"Great!" Summer wrote on the board: Saying kind words about effort. "What else?"

Jayden added. "Looking at someone when they're talking. Not at your desk."

"Excellent!" Summer added, "Giving full attention when someone is speaking." Then, she turned to the group. "Do you see what Jayden's doing here? He's helping us describe specific actions that match our intentions. Let's keep building."

Ideas poured in: clapping for classmates' successes, offering help when someone is struggling, noticing and naming others' unique strengths, and even organizing a class celebration for achievements. As Summer jotted them down, she grouped similar ideas and asked clarifying questions.

Next, they worked on inclusion. Summer kept the energy high this time, inviting students to call out ideas such as inviting people to play, ensuring no one is left out, and letting everyone have a say in group work. She added a final idea of her own: "Inclusion isn't just letting someone join; it's also making them feel truly welcome and wanted."

As the discussion wrapped up, Summer stepped back, reading the energy in the room. The clarity they had built together felt like a fresh breeze sweeping through the space. The air was light, essential, and life-giving. The list of actions on the board was the start of a blueprint for how they could intentionally honor each other's dignity in every interaction.

Just as plants take in carbon dioxide and release oxygen, the students took in the aspirations of their Dignity Promise and transformed them into specific, clear Dignity Expectations. They could breathe these in and exhale them as actions.

"Great work, everyone," Summer said, moving to her data projector. "Now, let's take this to the next level. We will create a four-point rubric describing what these expectations look like at different levels." She projected a familiar four-point chart on the screen, with columns labeled 1 to 4 and rows for Recognition and Inclusion.

"We'll start by describing what it looks like when doing these well. That's a 4. Then, we'll work backward to define when we're not doing so well, which is a 1. You and your partner will work with another pair to form groups of four. Sound good?"

Excitement flickered across the students' faces as they nodded.

Over the next two days, they co-created rubrics for Recognition, Inclusion, Acceptance, and Acknowledgment, writing them on large sheets of chart paper. They shared, critiqued, refined, and took ownership of the criteria, ensuring that what they created was theirs, and not something imposed on them. By the end of the second day, four completed rubrics were on display at the front of the room. Summer capped her marker and stepped back.

"We did it!" she said. "These Dignity Expectations will make our class stronger. They are the air we breathe. And we're going to use them every single day!"

By defining their expectations, Summer and her students co-created the clear, shared understanding necessary to bring their Dignity Promise to life. Now they knew exactly what was expected of them. But such clarity isn't automatic and, without it, even the best intentions can drift without direction, and then dissipate.

Defining Dignity Expectations

Let's leave Summer's classroom for now and examine her Dignity Expectations exercise through the lens of gardening. Plants need air. Without it, they can't grow or survive.[35] They use carbon dioxide to fuel photosynthesis, producing the energy they need to live. In our plant analogy, air represents Dignity Expectations, the invisible yet essential force that shapes how we live and interact. Like air, we don't usually see expectations, but they're always there, they're real, and their quality and clarity matter.

Just as air invisibly fills the environment, expectations invisibly fill a classroom. Expectations guide behavior, set norms, and can ensure dignity isn't just an abstraction but also a lived experience. Any lack of clear expectations is like trying to breathe in thin or polluted air. We will not be able to breathe and function well for long. No matter how strong our intentions are, a dignity-centered classroom won't flourish if students and teachers lack a shared understanding of what is expected of them.

For a real-life example, see Table 5.1, which displays an authentic set of Dignity Expectations created by Summer Snyder's 2022 second-grade class. First, the students identified the four dignity components most relevant to their classroom at that moment: Acceptance, Recognition, Acknowledgment, and Inclusion. Then, they co-created a four-point rubric, defining a continuum of behaviors for each category, from ideal (4) to unacceptable (1). These success criteria served as a shared roadmap for how they would actively uphold dignity in daily interactions.

---

35. And just like plants, classrooms can't thrive in a vacuum. Unless we're talking about the movie *Total Recall* starring Arnold Schwarzenegger. But even then, things didn't go so well without air. "Give these people air!"

TABLE 5.1

Dignity Expectations Example—Rubric

Code of Collaboration[36]				
	Inclusion	Acknowledgment	Recognition	Acceptance
1	Intentionally excluding others and choosing who gets to join.	Ignoring and walking away from others.	Saying hurtful things to others.	Being afraid to be yourself. Teasing or making fun of others.
2	Not allowing people to join in an activity.	Not giving your full attention when someone is talking to you.	Sometimes giving a compliment or thanking others.	Sometimes being brave. Sometimes teasing or making fun of others.
3	Inviting people to join and work, play, or interact with you.	Listening and apologizing for hurting others' feelings.	Congratulating others for doing a great job and recognizing their achievements.	Being proud of yourself and others around you.
4	Creating moments for all to be included.	Giving your full attention and repairing any harm.	Showing excitement for others' accomplishments.	Sticking up for others and celebrating our differences.
Note: Summer Snyder's second-grade classroom, 2022.				

---

36. We used to call it a Code of Conduct, but then Starla Watson, one of our partners from Yelm, Washington, came along and upgraded it, like when cassette tapes gave way to CDs. A Code of Collaboration just sounds better, doesn't it? Less compliance, more teamwork. Now, if only she could help us bring back the thrill of a good mixtape.

After reviewing this rubric, it's clear why this tool is so powerful. It provides

- explicit success criteria for preparing for interactions and self-reflection,

- a framework for setting behavioral goals and providing peer and teacher feedback, and

- a shared language to ensure dignity remains an ongoing practice, and does not become an abstract ideal.

We'll explore how to create and apply Dignity Expectations in more detail later. But first, let's examine the reason they matter so much.

The Power of Clarity

We can state the effectiveness of Dignity Expectations in one word: clarity. Without clarity, even the best intentions fall apart. Ambiguity leads to inconsistency, confusing students about what dignity looks like in action (even when they want to uphold it). Do your students know explicitly what it means to honor dignity in your classroom? Can they describe dignity in action? If not, it's time to make expectations clear, expressed, and shared.

In education, teacher clarity, a concept popularized by John Hattie (2023), refers to how clearly and effectively teachers communicate learning intentions, explain content, and outline success criteria during lessons. With an effect size of 0.75, teacher clarity is nearly twice as impactful as the average instructional strategy, making it one of the most powerful drivers of student achievement (Hattie, 2023). According to Hattie, teacher clarity helps students answer three essential questions:

1. What am I learning?

2. Why am I learning it?

3. How will I know when I've learned it?

We apply these principles to classroom culture. Dignity Expectations provide clarity by providing answers to these questions:

- ☑ What behaviors do we need as a community?
- ☑ Why are these behaviors important?
- ☑ How will we know if we're upholding them?

When expectations are vague or implied, students are left guessing what educators expect of them.[37] When expectations are explicit, however, students and teachers can engage with shared confidence. Furthermore, when they are explicit as well as co-created, every classroom community member can practice both responsibility and accountability for the expectations.

Unfortunately, many institutional efforts to promote dignity fall short because they lack this proactive precision.

From Compliance to Clarity

Most policies and legal frameworks attempt to define dignity by focusing on what not to do—outlining behaviors to avoid rather than providing clear, actionable guidance for what dignity looks like in practice. This negative focus is not sufficient. It's asking the wrong question. Most of us know what we shouldn't be doing. But do we know what we should be doing? Hmm. Probably not.

For example, New York State's Dignity for All Students Act (New York State Education Department, 2012) emphasizes prohibiting discrimination, ha-

---

37. "Where's the beef?" asked the elderly lady in the Wendy's commercial from the 1980s, when faced with a giant bun and a tiny burger patty. She wanted substance, a real burger, just like students need real clarity. Okay, maybe not just like that, but vague expectations don't help anyone.

rassment, and bullying in schools (New York State Education Department, 2012, Art. 2, §10). Similarly, the Constitution of the State of Illinois (1970, Art. I, § 20) includes a Bill of Rights with a section on Individual Dignity. It condemns hatred and abuse based on race, ethnicity, and other identities.

While these policies serve as critical guardrails against indignity and humiliation, they could do much more to contribute to the active cultivation of dignity-centered communities. We argue that rules about what not to do aren't enough.[38] Instead, in schools and classrooms, students and teachers need clear expectations that define what to do.

That's why Dignity Expectations are essential. Instead of merely prohibiting negative behaviors, they clarify how to honor dignity. Rather than imposing success criteria from the top down for students, co-creating them along with students shifts expectations from a compliance-based approach to a commitment-driven one. The result is a classroom culture where dignity isn't a rule to follow but a shared responsibility to uphold.

Co-Creating Expectations

We see this process at work in Summer's classroom scene at the beginning of this chapter. She helped her second-graders move beyond theoretical learning. After prioritizing specific components of dignity, Summer guided her students through translating those concepts into explicit, observable behaviors.

They generated ideas that ranged from simple phrases like, "Say kind words about effort" to specific actions, such as "Make sure no one feels

---

38. We know this well, having logged way too many hours watching 1980s movies. You know the trope: a rebellious teen gets a laundry list of what not to do, but zero guidance on what they should do. Which, of course, leads to questionable choices, an inevitable crisis, and a last-ditch effort to win back the town, the karate tournament, or the girl. Cue a heartfelt montage set to Kenny Loggins. Can you hear it? Bueller?

left out." As inspiring and hopeful as this exercise was, it would have remained a thought experiment and not a pragmatic tool if Summer and her students had stopped there. But they didn't stop; they continued synthesizing the behaviors and created a way to measure how well they were doing.

They co-created a four-point rubric (Figure 5.1) to define each expectation at different levels.[39] For example, in the Recognition category, students agreed that, at level 4, they would consistently notice and celebrate each other's strengths. In contrast, at level 2, they might only sometimes recognize their peers' efforts.

The process of co-creation helped ensure that Summer's students would walk the talk. They took ownership of their expected behaviors; these expectations weren't just statements posted on a wall, in a handbook, or in the school policy manual. They understood at a deeper level what went into honoring each other's dignity. Rather than just following rules they might or might not know the reasons for or even care about, Summer's students became active participants in shaping their classroom culture. That's precisely why this approach is so practical.

Research shows that co-created expectations support students' sense of belonging, ownership of the rules, respect for the rules, and collaborative problem-solving capabilities (Demir et al., 2023; Edutopia, 2019; Garrett, 1982; Hoyle & O'Connor, 2018). That's because they own and believe in them, which is far better than complying because they have to, "or else." When students help define dignity, they own it. When they own it, they

---

39. Never doubt that second graders are able to create quality rubrics with the proper guidance! If 1980s kids could roam the neighborhood unsupervised until the streetlights came on (not to mention outsmart government agents, build makeshift communication devices, and fly BMX bikes across a moonlit sky to save their alien best friend), today's second graders can definitely handle a rubric.

live it. And that's how dignity moves from an abstract concept to an everyday reality.

But this approach isn't just for second-graders!

It's (Not Just) Elementary: A Scalable Approach

This process worked beautifully in Summer's elementary classroom, but the same principles apply across all grade levels, even schoolwide or beyond. Dignity expectations can be developed by students, faculty, and staff in middle, high, and upper schools. The goal is to produce a departmental or school-wide Code of Collaboration.

Consider the example of digital citizenship expectations, a growing concern in today's classrooms. A school community might prioritize Safety or Accountability as key components for online interactions. To start the process, high school teachers might ask, "What does responsible online engagement look like?"

Through discussions and a broader goal (department or school) of consensus building, students might define specific behaviors, such as

- ☑ avoid writing negative comments on discussion boards, and
- ☑ cite sources when using artificial intelligence (AI) tools to write an assignment.

Teachers increase clarity and shared responsibility by engaging students in defining these behaviors, ensuring that digital norms are both relevant and meaningful.

Educators can apply the same approach in any environment, whether defining expectations for group work, classroom discussions, or school-wide initiatives. Perhaps we're stating the obvious, but it also applies to any organization, home, or community.

Specific Guidance for Creating Clear Expectations

Given the research, every educational system should equip teachers with the skills to develop clear behavioral expectations. These expectations form the very foundation of a safe and supportive learning environment, and studies consistently show that well-defined guidelines enhance engagement, encourage positive behavior, and contribute to academic success (Alter & Haydon, 2017).

The basic steps in developing expectations include these:

- **Prioritize three to five expectations** to keep them manageable.
- **Use positive language** to convey desired behaviors.
- **Balance general expectations with specific expectations** to promote shared understanding.
- **Teach and reteach expectations** to maintain clarity and consistency.

These steps probably seem familiar to you, since they align with well-established strategies for creating shared behavioral norms and expectations: classroom norms, social contracts, community agreements, guidelines, and so on. But Dignity Expectations go deeper. They extend beyond behavior management and establish a foundation for human connection. Rather than just outlining how students should behave, Dignity Expectations start with a shared understanding of dignity as a framework for how people should be treated and how they should treat others.

To establish Dignity Expectations, follow these three essential steps (Figure 5.1):

- **Teach** Dignity Content to students.

- **Learn** Dignity Needs from students.
- **Co-create** Dignity Expectations with students.

These three steps ensure educators lead with dignity (e.g., partnership, shared language) rather than relying on compliance (e.g., dominance, unilateral decisions).

FIGURE 5.1

Establishing Dignity Expectations

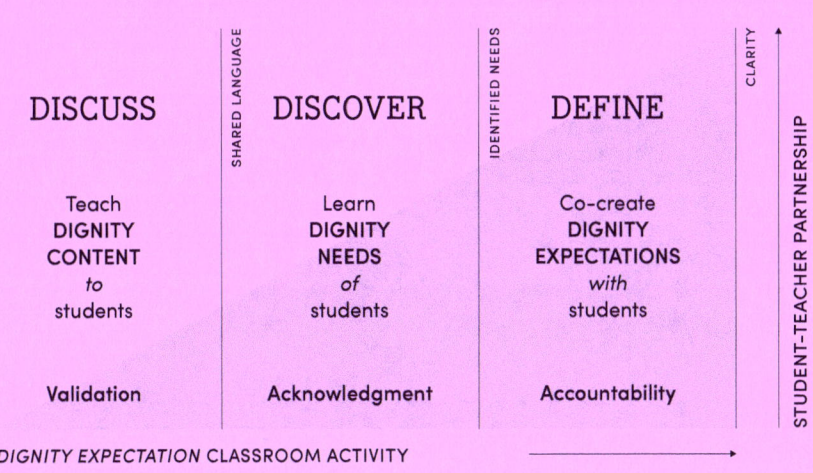

The first step is to teach: Ensure the community has a shared language to describe what humans need to feel like they matter and to be at their best. Table 5.2 provides an overview of the key components of dignity, which serve as the foundational reference points for co-created Dignity Expectations.

TABLE 5.2

Components of Dignity—What We Want and Need

Essentials	Standards	Dispositions	Indicators
Acceptance of identity	Build community and partnership	Listening	Appreciation
Accountability		Empathy	Validation
Acknowledg-ment	Repair harm and restore relationship	Patience	Connection
Benefit of the doubt	Affirm differences and uniqueness	Openness	Acceptance
Fairness			
Inclusion	Presume competence and positive intent		
Independence			
Recognition			
Safety			
Understanding			

Note: Summary of concepts from F. Cobb & J. Krownapple (2019) and D. Hicks (2018).

Next, teachers learn: They identify the components of dignity that matter most to students at a given time and place. For example, teachers can do this through surveys, dot voting, or multi-voting. Regardless of the method, the goal remains the same: prioritizing three to five components of dignity the community believes it needs to work on to keep its Dignity Promise. This groundwork sets the stage for creating success criteria. However, key considerations must come first.

Bridging Cultural Expectations

Before co-creating success criteria, it's essential to recognize that students and teachers bring diverse cultural experiences into the classroom (Austin, 2022). No one enters the learning space as a blank slate; various norms, values, and experiences shape how different people interpret expectations. Take the dignity element of safety, for example:

- In one student's home, safety might mean speaking calmly to avoid conflict.
- In another's, safety might mean speaking loudly to establish boundaries.

Expectations can feel unclear, misapplied, or even unfair without acknowledging these differences. That's why bridging personal experiences with shared Dignity Expectations is crucial. A well-facilitated process ensures that expectations are inclusive, relevant, and reflective of diverse perspectives (Muldrew & Miller, 2020).

A Tool to Build the Bridge

An effective tool for bridging cultural perspectives is the Personal Matrix Activity, also called a behavior dictionary (Leverson et al., 2021). Studies show that this clarifies expectations, fosters positive behavior, reduces disruptions, and decreases disproportionality in discipline data (Gion et al., 2021; Muldrew & Miller, 2021).

Teachers can use the behavior dictionary to prompt students to reflect on how key dignity components show up in different contexts (Table 5.3):

- At school
- At home
- In their neighborhood

By making these comparisons explicit, students recognize how expectations differ across environments and identify common threads that unify the class.

TABLE 5.3

Personal Matrix Activity (Behavior Dictionary)— Example

Dignity Component	At **school** it looks like...	At **home**, it looks like...	In my **neighbor-hood**, it looks like...
Recognition			
Acknowledgment			
Inclusion			
Note: Adapted from Leverson et al., 2021.			

Completing the Personal Matrix is just the first step. To deepen understanding, students need structured dialogue to process their insights. This helps the classroom community start bridging the gaps in expectations. Teachers can use discussion protocols, such as the Three-Step Interview (Table 5.4), to help students

☑ practice active listening,

☑ make connections between perspectives, and

☑ build shared understanding.

TABLE 5.4

Discussion Protocol Example

Name	Overview
Three Step Interview	Step 1: Student A interviews Student B.
	Step 2: Student B interviews Student A.
	Step 3: Students A and B summarize their interviews to another group
	Step 4: The teacher facilitates a debriefing.

Note: Summary of concepts based on Barkley et al., 2005.

These types of protocols are great for nurturing the Dignity Dispositions and are particularly valuable for students who might otherwise disengage due to a lack (or perceived lack) of belonging, agency, or skills. When done well, these conversations serve a trio of purposes. They

1. **create clarity**, helping students and teachers align on expectations,

2. **foster Dignity Dispositions**, nurturing listening, empathy, openness, and patience,[40] and

3. **strengthen relationships**, acting as Dignity Connectors that build trust and mutual respect.

Research on school discipline highlights why student involvement in shaping expectations is essential. Sean Austin (2022) argues that when students help create shared norms, they experience

---

40. The pre-internet world trained us in patience: waiting weeks for film rolls to develop, rewinding Blockbuster tapes, and sitting through a day of MTV just to catch *Thriller* again. Now, in 2025, youngsters don't even have to sit through an NFL game to glimpse Taylor Swift; everything they want to see is immediately available online, on demand. More than ever, patience is a disposition that's in dire need of intentional nurture in schools.

- ☑ greater ownership and **accountability**,
- ☑ stronger **relationships** with teachers, and
- ☑ increased **engagement** in learning.

He explains that co-creating norms "can convey a strong sense of compassion from teachers and support a mutual understanding that maintains clear boundaries and accountability for students and teachers" Austin (2022, p. 56). Research proves that working in partnership with students creates more-responsive and more-effective systems in classrooms, where teacher-imposed rules often dominate (Austin, 2022).

How to Co-Create Success Criteria

Creating Dignity Expectations is different from setting rules. It involves building a shared understanding of what dignity looks, sounds, and feels like in practice. To do this, students and teachers must first develop a shared sense of key dignity components.

This process begins with tools like the Personal Matrix Activity, which helps students surface different perspectives on dignity. Even at this early stage, students quickly realize that what feels natural to one person may be unfamiliar to another.

Examples:

- One student's idea of respect might be speaking quietly in class.
- Another student's idea of respect might be speaking directly and assertively.

Without clear and shared definitions, expectations become assumptions—and assumptions often lead to misunderstandings. That's why the next step is to co-construct descriptors, creating explicit statements that define how dignity is upheld in daily interactions.

For example, if recognition is a Dignity Expectation, a descriptor might be
☑ "We celebrate achievements, hard work, and thoughtfulness."

Once descriptors are developed, students and teachers collaborate to create rubrics that outline a continuum of behaviors from unacceptable to ideal (Table 5.5). This ensures that expectations are both measurable and meaningful.

TABLE 5.5

Sample Rubric for Recognition

Intention	1	2	3	4
Recognition	We ignore achievements, hard work, and thoughtfulness.	We sometimes notice good things people do.	We often acknowledge the good things people do.	We consistently celebrate achievements, hard work, and thoughtfulness.

By co-creating these criteria, students actively shape their classroom culture. Instead of simply following teacher-imposed rules, they take ownership of their agreements, making dignity a shared responsibility rather than a compliance-driven mandate.

How to Sustain Dignity Expectations

Establishing Dignity Expectations is a crucial first step, but it's vital to ensure that they stay relevant, actionable, and alive in the daily rhythm of the classroom. Without such mindful reinforcement, expectations can stagnate and lose credibility. When students don't see them in practice, dignity shifts from an active commitment to an empty slogan. Inconsistency breeds disengagement. If you don't act with dignity and model the expectations, students may look elsewhere for behavioral cues, likely in ways that undermine the classroom culture you're trying to build.

A true commitment to dignity means treating these expectations as living agreements, not fixed rules. Dignity Expectations can guide the following:

- ☑ Reflection: "To what degree are we upholding our shared expectations?"
- ☑ Goal setting: "How can we strengthen our behaviors and practices?"
- ☑ Feedback: "How do we support one another in meeting these expectations?"
- ☑ Conflict Resolution: "How do we repair harm when dignity is violated?"

For example, during times of interpersonal conflict, Summer helped students de-escalate by returning to their rubric. Revisiting their Dignity Promise and Expectations grounded the situation in their shared agreements, providing a path forward that prevented emotional reactions from running roughshod over the classroom. Their Dignity Expectations became a stabilizing force, offering clarity and consistency in how to navigate disagreements.

But just like a gardener adjusts to changing weather and soil conditions, classroom communities must periodically revisit and reassess their expectations. If students find certain expectations to be unclear or ineffective, they should refine them. If new challenges emerge, expectations should evolve to meet them. Also, once the community reaches consistent proficiency levels with them, it may be time to reassess and choose other components of dignity to focus on.

- Healthy plants don't thrive on neglect. They need ongoing attention, adjustments, and care.

- Classroom communities are no different. Expectations should be revisited, refined, and strengthened over time.

Your Next Step

Dignity Expectations provide the air that sustains a classroom's culture. But plants need more than sunlight, water, and air. They also need soil. The soil is our actions or what we call Dignity Actions. Without putting expectations into action, the expectations are just so many words that are insubstantial and potentially hypocritical. Dignity classrooms embody behaviors, practices, and policies that honor dignity. Dignity Actions are the norm. Just as plants need nourishing soil, students (and teachers) thrive through the actions of daily behaviors, choices, and interactions that bring their Dignity Expectations to life.

Look at how much we've covered so far. When it comes to understanding how to teach with dignity, you've learned how to establish the sunlight. You've sustained the water flow. You've ensured that air is circulating and doing its part to support a culture of dignity. Now, it's time to prepare the soil to support plant life.

In the next chapter, we'll dig into the ground of Dignity Actions, the small, everyday choices that transform dignity from an idea into a lived classroom reality.[41]

Grab your shovel. It's time to dig deep.

------

41. Cue the dramatic 1980s training montage music. *Eye of the Tiger*, anyone? We're about to get serious about action.

CHAPTER 6

Dignity Actions (Soil)

How wonderful it is that nobody need wait a single moment before starting to improve the world.

—Anne Frank, 1947/1995

Enriching the Soil Through Accountability

Summer felt like a pressure cooker about to blow. It was one of those dreaded school days in late May—just before summer vacation—when everyone, teachers included, was barely holding it together. The fresh air, sunlight, and sparkling green grass outside the windows were calling the students' names. Summer Snyder's second graders weren't just ready for summer—they were mentally already there.

All day long, they'd been restless, and worse. Talking over her. Squirming during lessons. Pushing limits. Her usual strategies of proximity, reminders, and quiet signals had lost their magic. The students in the back row, who'd been jabbing each other with pencils all morning, ignored her third request to stop.

Suddenly, Summer snapped.

"Stop it! Stop it right now! You are the worst class I've ever had!"

Immediately, pin-drop stunned silence.

Ava, who'd been leading the back-row pencil antics moments ago, now sat frozen, blinking back tears. Ethan, usually quick with a joke, inspected his nails like they held the universe's secrets. The entire room had shifted.

Summer's stomach dropped. What had she just done?

Horrified at her explosion, she turned to the blackboard and wrote to-morrow's homework assignment, even though it wasn't time to do that yet. She chose to soldier on stoically through the school day as if nothing had happened. She ignored Ava's stifled sob from the back row.

But that evening, sitting on her couch, Summer cradled a cup of tea that did absolutely nothing to comfort her. The image of her students' hurt faces haunted her. Her words echoed in her mind, cruel and irreversible.

"How could I have said that?" she whispered into the empty room.

She imagined what she'd feel like if a teacher spoke that way to her own child. The thought sickened her. Just as sickening, she'd spent all year building a dignity classroom with other people's children, and in one moment of anger, she'd crashed it all.

What to do now? She could continue to pretend it never happened, as teachers had done for generations. But she knew better. It had happened. Her students wouldn't forget.

Years ago, she'd probably have rationalized her outburst: *They weren't listening. They pushed me too far. I was exhausted.* Or worse, she might have given the classic non-apology, justifying her lousy behavior: *I'm sorry I yelled,* but *you weren't following directions.* That's not accountability, though. She knew that now. That's not caring for them, herself, dignity, or the promise they made to one another. That wasn't who she wanted to be anymore.

First thing the following day, she sat the class down on the rug. The students fidgeted, squirmed, and avoided meeting her eyes. They seemed unsure whether they were in trouble. Summer took a deep breath and began.

"Yesterday, I said something hurtful and unkind. I said you were the worst class I've ever had. That was wrong of me, and I'm so sorry."

A few students glanced at each other.

"Yesterday was tough. We all want summer vacation to start. We were all feeling frustrated, and I let my frustration get the better of me. That wasn't your fault. It's not true that you're the worst class I've ever had. I love being your teacher. My job was to stay calm and respectful, and I didn't. I'm going to work on being better. I hope you can forgive me."

Silence hung heavy for a few seconds that seemed like an eternity.

Then, a small voice said sharply, "Yeah, you broke our Dignity Promise."

Another voice, softer. "But we forgive you, Ms. Snyder." A ripple of nods and quiet smiles spread through the group. The air felt lighter.

At the end of the day, Summer found a note from a student on her desk. "Dear Ms. Snyder, yesterday you made a mistake, but today you made it better. That's what you always tell us to do, right? Love, Layla."

That evening, she received several messages from parents thanking her for modeling accountability. From that day forward, the classroom felt different. The students were more patient with each other, more understanding, and more willing to say "I'm sorry" when they messed up.

On that no-good, horrible day when Summer blew her stack, everyone (including Summer) learned something powerful. Dignity isn't about perfection. Dignity is about what we do next.

Actions as Soil

Summer's apology did more than mend the moment: it also restored health to the classroom soil. Through acknowledgment, accountability, and fairness, she replenished the nutrients sustaining their culture of dignity. Just as a gardener corrects imbalances in the soil, she recognized depleted essentials and took action to restore them.

Dignity isn't a slogan on the wall. It's a daily choice, especially in the most challenging moments. Had Summer ignored her outburst or brushed it off with a half-hearted excuse, she would have sent a message: our Dignity Promise is just words.

Nothing erodes a culture of dignity faster than hypocrisy.[42] If she'd let herself off the hook, she would have failed to repair the harm and modeled the exact behavior she wanted to prevent. Her actions would have carried more

---

42. See also: that moment in *The Karate Kid* when Cobra Kai dojo, known for its "No Mercy" philosophy, reacts with outrage when the tables turn—exposing the hypocrisy behind their selectively applied code.

weight than any lecture on dignity and respect ever could. What teachers do matters far more than what teachers say when shaping culture.

The word "culture" itself comes from agriculture. The Latin word "cultura" means to cultivate, tend, and grow (Harper, n.d.). Just as the quality of the soil determines the strength of the plants, a classroom's culture shapes the behaviors of its students.

Simply put, a classroom's culture is "the way we do things around here" (Bower, 1966, p. 112). And while each student plays a part in shaping it, the teacher's influence is foundational. The same dynamic applies at every level: Principals shape school culture, superintendents influence district culture, and so on. As educational leadership experts Steve Gruenert and Todd Whitaker (2015, p. 10) put it, "The culture of any [classroom] is shaped by the worst behavior the [teacher] is willing to tolerate."

That includes the teacher's behavior.

Summer's mistake didn't destroy the classroom culture, but how she followed up could have. By choosing authenticity over ego, and accountability over avoidance, she proved that dignity wasn't just an expectation for her students but a commitment for everyone.

As teachers, we can't just demand that people honor dignity (at least not successfully).[43] It has to be something we embody. A teacher who consistently models dignity is the strongest safeguard against humiliation, fear, and exclusion in a classroom.

———

43. Demanding dignity is like demanding someone relax. It kind of defeats the purpose. True dignity-centered action, like true relaxation, happens when it's modeled, not mandated.

Summer's bad day reinforced the fact that honoring dignity goes above and beyond being outwardly warm and establishing a welcoming environment, which can be relatively easy. Honoring dignity requires internal toughness. Internal toughness requires self-discipline, the kind needed when frustration peaks and patience wears thin. That's precisely what's required when the going gets tough.

Principles of dignity, such as accountability and fairness, must be woven into the fabric of classroom life to serve as the default response in the most challenging moments. Ultimately, teachers influence the classroom environment by tending its soil through words, behaviors, practices, policies, and, yes, even apologies when necessary.

How to Cultivate the Soil

Building a dignity-centered classroom takes intentional action—lots of it: deliberate choices and behaviors that nurture an environment where everyone feels valued. Gardeners don't simply scatter seeds and hope for the best. They prepare the soil, enrich it with nutrients, and monitor conditions to sustain healthy growth.

Teachers cultivate dignity by embedding consistent, intentional actions into daily routines. These actions do more than shape individual interactions; they establish dignity as a classroom expectation, not just an occasional act of kindness.

The Blueprint for Cultivating Dignity (Figure 6.1) provides a practical framework for embedding dignity into teacher behaviors and professional practices. Adapted from existing dignity frameworks (Cobb & Krownapple, 2019; Hicks, 2018), this model reimagines dignity-centered actions as what sustains a thriving learning environment.

FIGURE 6.1

Blueprint for Cultivating Dignity

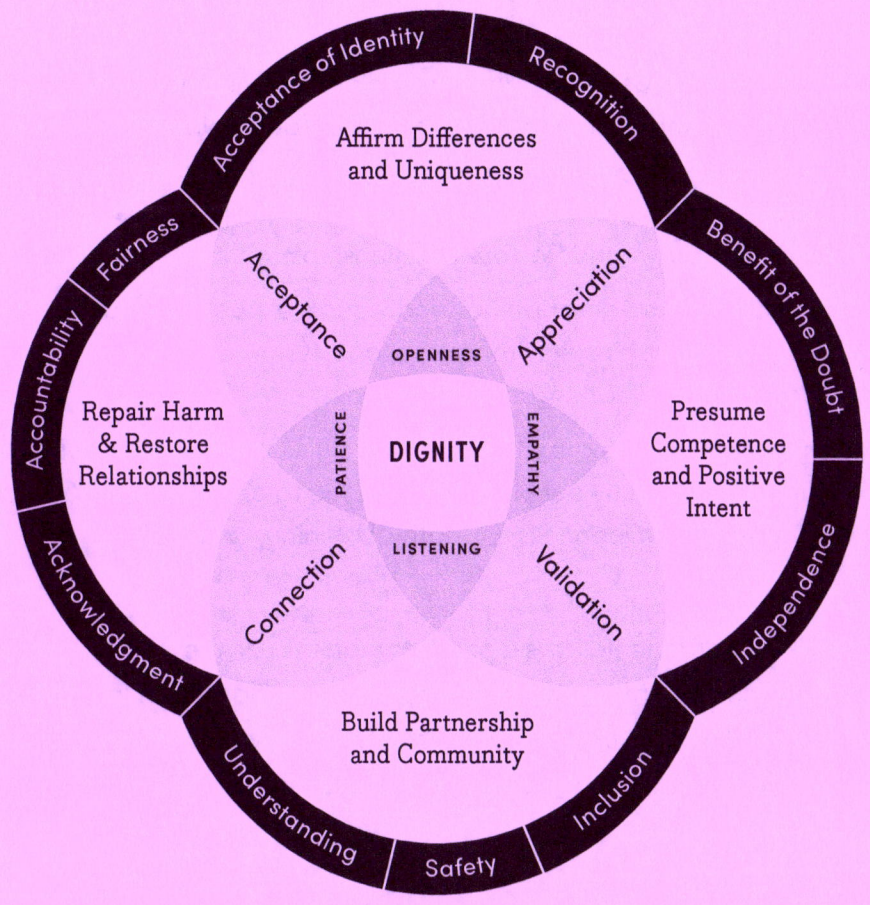

Note: Adapted from *Belonging Through a Culture of Dignity* (p. 111), by F. Cobb & J. Krownapple, 2019, Mimi & Todd Press. Copyright 2019 by Floyd Cobb and John Krownapple. Also adapted from *Leading with Dignity* (pp. 16–17), by D. Hicks, 2018, Yale University Press. Copyright 2018 by Donna Hicks. Adapted with permission.

Moving from the outer edge of the Blueprint to its center, its components are these:

⊘ **Dignity Essentials** are the foundational human needs required for individuals to feel their dignity is honored (Hicks, 2018): Acceptance of Identity, Recognition, Benefit of the Doubt, Independence, Inclusion, Safety, Understanding, Acknowledgment, Accountability, and Fairness.

- ⌀ **Dignity Standards** are guiding principles that ensure dignity is consistently upheld in behaviors, practices, and policies (Cobb & Krownapple, 2019): Affirm Differences and Uniqueness, Presume Competence and Positive Intent, Build Partnerships and Community, and Repair Harm and Restore Relationships.

- ⌀ **Dignity Indicators** describe how individuals experience dignity through relationships, environments, and systems: Acceptance, Appreciation, Validation, and Connection.

- ⌀ **Dignity Dispositions** are the internal qualities that guide people's ability to consistently act in ways that honor dignity (Cobb & Krownapple, 2019): Openness, Empathy, Listening, and Patience.

Much like a gardener follows a planting plan to cultivate a thriving landscape, teachers can use this Blueprint to design classroom interactions that create the conditions for growth. Consistency in everyday actions, both big and small, becomes the nutrient-rich soil within which students can thrive.

Dignity in Action: Beyond Relationships

Teaching with dignity embeds dignity-centered action into every dimension of teaching. Fostering positive interpersonal relationships is essential, but is not enough. Dignity Actions are needed. These actions are embedded in classroom policies, instructional choices, and the learning environment. They shape the students' sense of worth, belonging, and agency.

To help structure this process, we draw from scholars of belonging, De-Leon Gray and colleagues (2018), who identify three key dimensions for teacher action. We've added a fourth dimension, intrapersonal, and then present these four focus areas for embedding dignity-centered action into the classroom culture.

1. **Intrapersonal:** Helping students honor their self-worth and develop self-awareness (e.g., self-regulation, self-efficacy).

2. **Interpersonal:** Strengthening positive social connectedness between teachers and students, and among students.

3. **Institutional:** Designing policies, practices, and procedures to reinforce dignity throughout the school day.

4. **Instructional:** Making strategic decisions about teaching methods and materials that promote a dignity-centered learning experience.

Table 6.1 provides practical examples of dignity in action across these dimensions. The examples illustrate how honoring dignity can become the cultural norm that anchors and nourishes students and teachers.

TABLE 6.1

Examples of Dignity as Action in the Classroom

Dignity Standard	Dignity Essential
Presume Competence and Positive Intent	Benefit of the Doubt
	Independence
Build Partnerships and Community	Inclusion
	Safety
	Understanding
Repair Harm and Restore Relationship	Acknowledgment
	Accountability
	Fairness
Affirm Differences and Uniqueness	Acceptance of Identity
	Recognition

Examples			
Intrapersonal	**Interpersonal**	**Institutional**	**Instructional**
Teach students to trust themselves.	Use positive pre-suppositions.	Offer a rigorous curriculum.	Provide growth-oriented feedback.
Facilitate student goal setting.	Foster peer collaboration.	Delegate class-room roles and responsibilities.	Make room for student voice and choice.
Establish student self-affirmation exercises.	Greet students.	Co-create class-room vision.	Design collabora-tive learning experiences.
Teach emotional awareness.	Talk at eye level.	Clear & consistent expectations.	Model and normalize mistakes.
Have students authentically learn about themselves.	Normalize active listening.	Hold routine class meetings & check-ins.	Use discussion protocols.
Normalize learning from mistakes.	Model apologizing for mistakes.	Implement conflict -resolution protocols.	Use student input to adapt instruc-tion.
Teach self-accountability.	Right wrongs.	Implement feedback systems.	Ensure instruct-ional scaffolds.
Teach self-compassion.	Ensure equal treat-ment without favoritism.	Integrate restor-ative practices.	Use Every Pupil Response (EPR) techniques.
Implement strength mapping activities.	Pronounce names correctly.	Ensure classroom materials provide representation.	Ensure the rele-vance of materials.
Use achievement and gratitude journals.	Provide and normalize appre-ciative feedback.	Have rituals for celebrating behaviors & results.	Celebrate acdemic progress.

Simple But Not Easy

First, do no harm. It sounds simple, right? But simple isn't the same as easy.

It's relatively easy to align behaviors, practices, and policies with dignity expectations when everyone is calm and well-rested. But what about when frustration builds? When students test limits? When exhaustion frays patience to the breaking point?[44] These are the moments when dignity is hardest to uphold and when it matters most.

Think about Summer Snyder's moment of frustration. She knew better. She had spent a career building a reputation as a master teacher, and she worked all year to cultivate trust, nurture belonging, and shape a safe and supportive classroom culture. Yet her actions seemed to undo it all in one moment of exhaustion and exasperation.

This scenario is all too familiar. Lower instincts take the wheel when stress, fatigue, or frustration take over. Instead of responding thoughtfully, people react emotionally. As Donna Hicks (2018, p. 30) describes, they succumb to the "temptations to violate dignity" (Table 6.2). Whether it's taking the bait, playing the victim, or shifting blame, these reactive behaviors erode trust and cause harm, even when there's no bad intent.[45]

Why This Is Hard

At their core, these temptations are defense mechanisms. Like pointy thorns on a rose, they're designed to protect vulnerability but are capable of causing unintended harm (Figure 6.2).

---

44. Also known as "teaching the day after an all-night *Stranger Things* binge on Netflix."

45. Poison ivy doesn't care if you didn't mean to touch it. Like unintentional dignity violations, intent is irrelevant. If you don't learn to recognize the leaves, you'll find out the hard way. By then, the damage is done and likely spreading.

TABLE 6.2

Hicks's Temptations to Violate Dignity

1. **Take the bait.** Letting someone's bad behavior provoke an emotional response aimed at getting even.

2. **Save face.** Lying to cover up or deceive others to prevent looking bad.

3. **Shirk responsibility.** Refusing to own mistakes and shifting blame to someone else.

4. **Seek false dignity.** Tying self-worth to external validation rather than intrinsic value.

5. **Seek false security.** Remaining in relationships or environments where your dignity is routinely violated.

6. **Avoid conflict.** Failing to stand up for oneself and others when dignity is violated.

7. **Be the victim.** Refusing to acknowledge one's role in conflict and claiming innocence in failed relationships.

8. **Resist feedback.** Rejecting input that could support personal growth.

9. **Blame and shame others.** Deflecting guilt and instead making someone else look bad.

10. **Gossip and false intimacy.** Talking negatively about others to bond with people.

Note: Adapted from *Leading with Dignity* (pp. 31–323), by D. Hicks, 2018, Yale University Press. Copyright 2018 by Donna Hicks. Adapted with permission.

FIGURE 6.2

Cautionary Guide for Recognizing the Violation of Dignity

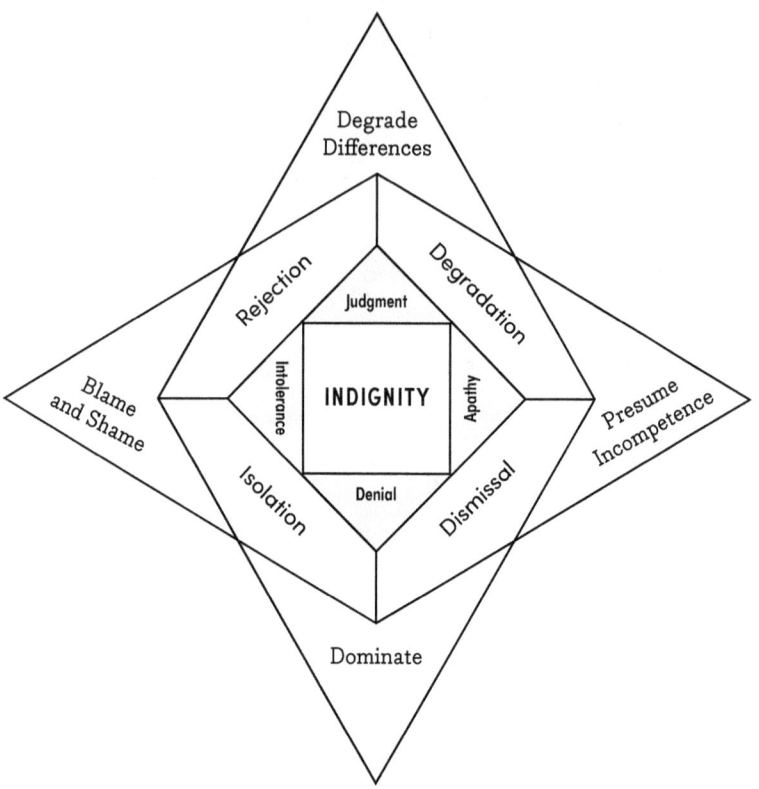

Note: Adapted from *Belonging Through a Culture of Dignity* (p. 144), by F. Cobb & J. Krownapple, 2019, Mimi & Todd Press. Copyright 2019 by Floyd Cobb and John Krownapple.

In the moment, harmful behavior (dignity violations) can feel justified. It may seem reasonable to think, "They pushed me to this point" or "They left me no other option."[46] Like failing to recognize poison ivy before

---

46. Fun fact: This is also the internal monologue of every parent who's ever confiscated an iPad.

touching it, though, not identifying dignity violations early on can lead to painful consequences. If you don't learn to spot the signs, especially in your behavior as a teacher, you risk being harmed or, worse, allowing them to spread unchecked. They'll take over the classroom before you even realize what has happened.

Consider a teacher who perceives a student as acting disrespectfully. The teacher takes the bait and responds with sarcasm or a harsh reprimand. The student, feeling attacked, doubles down in defiance, reinforcing the very behavior the teacher was trying to correct. In the worst cases, the student might even adopt the same reactionary habits, justifying bad behavior by pointing back at the teacher: "Well, you started it!"

Left unchecked, these moments accumulate, reshaping the classroom environment in subtle but significant ways. Defensiveness replaces accountability. Fear replaces trust. Frustration replaces connection. That's why recognizing and managing dignity violations is critical for anyone committed to teaching with dignity (Figure 6.2).[47]

Responding vs. Reacting

At its core, teaching with dignity is about responding, not reacting. The difference? A reaction is automatic, driven by emotion and impulse. A response is intentional. It's fortified by self-awareness, self-regulation, and a commitment to honoring dignity, even in difficult moments.

This distinction is crucial because every classroom has a tipping point. Ultimately, the culture of a learning environment is shaped by what

---

47. As a teacher, your dignity violations are like *Gremlins*. If you don't catch them early, they multiply into chaos. Rule #1: Don't feed them, after midnight or at all, unless you want a full-blown culture of indignity on your hands.

teachers and students do, and not what they say they will do, even in their most stressed moments.

- If they uphold dignity only when it's easy, it's a convenience, not a commitment.
- If they allow violations of dignity when times are hard, it signals that rules aren't real, trust is illusionary, belonging is conditional, and fairness is inconsistent.

The test of a classroom culture of dignity is how everyone (teachers and students) handles mistakes, conflict, and stress.

As such, self-awareness and self-management lie at the heart of teaching with dignity, starting with the teacher. What happens within people is just as important as what happens between people, if not more so. Recognizing personal vulnerabilities allows individuals to pause, regulate, and choose dignity-centered responses over knee-jerk reactions.

Vulnerable Decision Points

It's relatively easy to honor dignity when everything is going well.[48] But we know that's not real life. So how do educators train themselves to respond with dignity under pressure, when frustration, stress, exhaustion, or fear take over? When your own no-good, horrible day comes knocking?

The reality is that everyone has moments of vulnerability, times when emotions override rational thinking. Educational research refers to these moments as vulnerable decision points (VDPs) (Smolkowski et al., 2016).

---

48. Just ask the 1986 New York Mets, unstoppable when winning, a disaster when not. Hernandez chain-smoking, Dykstra wrecking cars, Strawberry throwing punches, and Gooden vanishing for days. Ultimately, poor Billy Buckner must have absorbed that energy when that infamous World Series ground ball found its way through his legs.

VDPs occur when two factors collide:

1. a **specific situation** that increases the risk of a reactionary response, and

2. an **internal state** (e.g., stress, fatigue, frustration) that lowers a person's ability to respond thoughtfully.

At these moments, dignity is at its most fragile. Educators and students alike are more likely to break their Dignity Promises and fall short of their Dignity Expectations. It's not because they want or intend to, but because they're emotionally compromised. Recognizing VDPs is the first step in preventing these harmful missteps.

Research has revealed predictable patterns in VDPs. Smolkowski and colleagues (2016) found that teachers are particularly vulnerable to reactionary responses when

- **they feel** unsupported or exhausted,

- **the lesson** design lacks engagement, leading to disruptive student behavior, and when

- **they perceive** student behavior as disrespectful, especially in subjective situations.

Building on this, Dr. Sean Austin (2022) identified key trends:

- The majority of VDPs occur inside the classroom.

- Defiance and disruption are the most common behavioral triggers.

- These moments contribute significantly to disparities in school discipline, particularly along racial and gender lines.

This research underscores a crucial truth: When teachers subjectively judge student behavior, the risk of bias and inconsistency increases (Gregory & Weinstein, 2008).

Take, for example, a teacher who unilaterally decides that a student is being rude and uncooperative. In a moment of stress, frustration, or exhaustion, this judgment is likely informed by bias, leading to reactions that can undermine trust and harm students.

But here's the good news: VDPs are not inevitable disasters. You can anticipate and navigate them. Understanding personal VDP patterns isn't about self-criticism but rather strategic preparation. Sometimes it's as simple as discovering that hunger depletes patience at a specific time of day and packing a snack to intervene.[49] Identifying when and why these moments occur allows educators to respond intentionally instead of reacting impulsively. Just as gardeners plan for changing seasons, educators can equip themselves with strategies to uphold dignity when emotions are likely to run high.

We Are Wired to Violate Dignity

If upholding dignity were simply a matter of knowing better, dignity violations wouldn't be so common. But wanting to do the right thing and being able to in the moment are very different. The reason? Human biology and psychology.

When a person experiences stress, the brain activates its fight-or-flight reaction. This automatic survival mechanism protects against danger. However, it often does more harm than good in a classroom, where the perceived threat might be any number of things: the teacher's perception of a defiant student, an off-task class, a chaotic lesson, students behaving in a way that reinforces stereotypes, or being judged incompetent.

Under stress, the brain prioritizes instinct over reason. The prefrontal

---

49. Pro tip: Keep emergency snacks in your desk. The difference between a meltdown and a mindful response is sometimes 200 calories.

cortex, which is responsible for rational thinking, impulse control, and emotional regulation, becomes less effective, while the amygdala, which governs instinctive reactions, takes over (Arnsten, 2009). This shift makes people more likely

- **to react rather than respond**, by snapping, yelling, or punishing impulsively;
- **to misinterpret intent**, assuming a student is being disrespectful when they are instead anxious or confused, or
- **to fall back on biases**, relying on stereotypes when making quick judgments.

Research by Keinan, Friedland, and Even-Haim (2000) shows that stress increases reliance on cognitive shortcuts, including both helpful and harmful biases. However, when teachers have broad discretion over what they count as defiance or disruption, dignity violations are more likely (Owens & McLanahan, 2020).

The Perfect Storm for Dignity Violations

Imagine an educator running on four hours of sleep, overwhelmed by grading, who hasn't had a break or eaten much all day. A student loudly and negatively reacts to a direction. On a good day, the teacher might de-escalate the situation with curiosity. But under stress, the teacher's brain registers the defiance as a threat, and the teacher reacts, perhaps with a harsh reprimand, a sarcastic remark, or a disciplinary referral.

This moment is a textbook VDP. The teacher's internal state (exhaustion) collides with a specific situation (a student's loud reaction). When these factors align, dignity violations become more likely.

Research offers clear insights for educators committed to fostering a culture of dignity:

- ☑ Stress and fatigue increase the likelihood of reactive, indignant responses.

- ☑ Subjective judgments of student behavior amplify the risk of harmful biases.

- ☑ Dignity violations disproportionately harm students who are already most vulnerable.

- ☑ Failing to acknowledge and repair dignity violations undermines classroom trust.

These findings reinforce an essential truth: Teaching with dignity is far more than knowing what to do when things are going well. It also requires self-preparation for the inevitable moments when it's most difficult to honor dignity and be your best self.

How to Maintain Dignity in Tough Times

Recognizing VDPs is the first step. The more-significant challenge lies in navigating VDPs in the moment, choosing dignity-centered responses rather than defaulting to reactive responses. While VDPs may be inevitable, research provides practical strategies to mitigate their impact and reduce the likelihood of dignity violations.

A common but flawed assumption is that racial bias alone drives racial disparities in discipline (Austin, 2022). While harmful biases may play a role, research consistently shows that multiple factors shape VDPs, including stress, fatigue, and school policies. This misconception about racial bias has fueled the largely ineffective approach to train out bias in professional development (Sparks, 2020). Instead, educators can invest in working to prioritize strategies that build self-awareness, regulate emotions, and support dignity-centered responses. Here are some steps you can take on your own.

1. **Engage in self-reflection.** The ability to uphold dignity in challenging moments begins with honest self-reflection. Pondering ques-

tions such as these can help you recognize areas for growth:

- Have I expected these dignifying actions of myself? If not, why not?
- Why aren't dignity-centered practices the standard in every school?
- What prevents educators from using dignity-centered strategies consistently with all students?

2. **Identify personal triggers.** Self-awareness is key. Every educator has their own hot buttons, situations that make maintaining a healthy response difficult, including

- **certain student behaviors** (defiance, eye-rolling, disengagement);
- **specific times of day** (before lunch, after recess, end of the day); and
- **recurring classroom challenges** (students not following directions, lack of participation).

Gathering feedback from colleagues, reviewing disciplinary data (e.g., SWIS [School-Wide Information System] reports), or reflecting on student interactions can help identify patterns. Once you recognize your triggers, you can better prepare to respond.

3. **Plan a dignity-centered response.** Once you identify triggers, the next step is adopting a neutralizing routine (Table 6.3), a simple strategy that interrupts automatic reactions and fosters intentional, dignity-centered responses (McIntosh, et al., 2014).[50] The most effective routines are clear, quick, and actionable:

- ☑ **Clear:** Easy to remember in high-pressure moments
- ☑ **Quick:** Can be used immediately in the classroom
- ☑ **Actionable:** Provides specific steps to follow

---

50. Reacting: *Ms. Pac Man* chasing every ghost. Responding: knowing when to wait for the power pellet.

TABLE 6.3

Five Essential Components of Neutralizing Routines

Component	Description	Example
If-then statement	Provides a clear course of action in response to a trigger.	If a student refuses directions, I will stay calm and say, "Let's talk privately."
Brief reminder	Is short enough to recall in high-pressure situations.	I will respond by doing these three things.
Clear steps	Is simple, specific, and easy to implement.	Take two breaths. Ask a question. Reflect something I heard.
Doable move	Is practical enough to apply in various classroom settings.	If a student is off task, I will walk closer to them, using proximity as a strategy.
Action that interrupts the chain of events	Creates a pause to prevent emotional escalation.	I will take a deep breath and remind myself that I have the power to uphold dignity in this moment.

Note: Summary of table content adapted from K. McIntosh (2019), *Neutralizing routines: Strategies to interrupt snap-judgment responses for staff and students*, presented at the California PBIS Conference.

4. **Practice neutralizing routines.** Like any habit, teachers must practice neutralizing routines to make them automatic. Research shows these strategies slow down impulsive decision-making, reducing the likelihood of dignity violations (Cook, Duong, et al., 2018).[51]

   - **T.R.Y.**—Take a breath, Reflect on emotions, and respond to Youth's best interest (McIntosh et al., 2021).

---

51. Think about reading a triggering email. A well-timed pause (ranging from a deep breath to a night of sleep) before hitting "Reply to All" has saved many careers.

- **S.T.O.P.**—Stop automatic reactions, Take two mindful breaths, Observe emotions, and Proceed positively (Renshaw et al., 2015).

- **P.A.R.**—Pause and reflect, Ask what the behavior is communicating, and Respond with listening and validation (National Center for Pyramid Innovations, 2023).

Additionally, a schoolwide approach to neutralizing routines positively impacts school culture and student outcomes. According to research by Santiago-Rosario and McIntosh (2021), shared routines

- ☑ increase consistency in positive student experiences in school,

- ☑ reduce stigmatization of individual staff members opting out of training, and

- ☑ ensure broader engagement of all school personnel (e.g., nurses, bus drivers, substitutes) in fostering a culture of dignity.

To capture the essence of neutralizing routines, consider the **H.U.M.B.L.E.** acronym. While not a step-by-step routine, it serves as a symbolic reminder of the mindset necessary for teaching with dignity. It aligns with the Dignity Dispositions (Figure 6.1): Listening, Empathy, Openness, and Patience.

- **H**elp, don't harm.

- **U**nderstand your triggers.

- **M**indfully practice patience.

- **B**e open.

- **L**isten actively.

- **E**mpathically respond.

Fear-Based Control: When the Soil Is Neglected

When educators and systems don't prioritize dignity in action, something else takes root: control (and dominance). Control, when driven by fear, may undermine everything educators work to build. In the garden, soil does more than anchor the plants; it also provides the nutrients needed for growth. However, neglected soil in a garden eventually loses its ability to sustain life. Plants may grow but are weak and sickly; opportunistic weeds invade and can take over, robbing the plants of what nutrients are available. The same is true in classrooms, metaphorically speaking.

Because traditional schooling often normalizes compliance cultures,[52] students often obey first and think later. Research shows that educators frequently use fear appeals (Putwain & von der Embse, 2018) to drive behavior: warnings about failure, punishment, or exclusion. These tactics can yield short-term obedience, but at a cost: they replace intrinsic motivation with anxiety, along with other negative mental states. Fear fills the gap of neglected dignity. Instead of a classroom where students feel safe to take risks, they learn to comply out of self-preservation. Instead of fostering growth, fear stifles it.

Just as a gardener enriches the soil to sustain a flourishing garden, educators can fortify the classroom culture through their behaviors. When they model vulnerability, humility, and dignity, teachers do not lose authority but gain positive influence (Bullough, 2005). A classroom culture fortified through dignity nurtures trust, accountability, and resilience.

Soil and Space for Growth

Like fertile soil, Dignity Actions provide the essential nutrients students need to grow. But even rich soil can't help a root-bound plant—a healthy plant trapped in a pot that does not provide sufficient room to expand. (Our gardening analogy includes plants in pots as well as plants in the ground.) That root-bound plant will struggle and probably end up stunted. The same is

---

52. A method also used by Blockbuster, whose rental policy for Video Home System (VHS) cassettes required customers to rewind them before returning. Be kind, rewind... or else be fined.

true for students. Without enough room to grow, they won't thrive.

In a garden, sufficient space is necessary for survival. In the ground, overcrowded plants don't just struggle—they also compete for resources, sometimes overshadowing or stunting one another's growth. A classroom without sufficient space (a Dignity Ecosystem) can create the same unfortunate dynamic, where students compete for affirmation, belonging, and power. This stifles collaboration and fosters hierarchies of worth where only a select few feel genuinely valued.

A culture of dignity ensures that everyone (teachers and students alike) has the psychological space to take risks, ask questions, disagree, speak up honestly, navigate challenges, and learn from mistakes. A well-designed ecosystem offers room for every person to expand their potential. Growth is a shared pursuit, not just an individual one. This includes the teacher's growth.

Your Next Step

Just as a gardener repots a plant when it outgrows its pot, teachers must expand learning conditions as students develop. If a structure is limiting growth, it must evolve. For example, educators can use a simple feedback loop after a lesson or unit, such as this Three-Rs protocol.[53] This iterative process encourages continuous improvement in teaching practices, fostering a classroom culture of dignity:

- **Review:** Assess the lesson's outcomes and gather data on your students' experiences, including belonging, engagement, and understanding.
- **Reflect:** Analyze the alignment of your instructional approach with

---

53. Shout out to Abe Villanueva in Pearl City, Hawai'i—educator, football coach, and the kind of guy who could've coached the *Mighty Ducks* and taught summer school. He brought "Review, Reflect, Revise" into John's playbook, proving that great protocols are like great teams: they provide the safety and structure to look within and get better.

your Dignity Expectations. Identify strengths and areas for improvement.

- **Revise:** Implement changes to your instructional approach based on insights gained from the review and reflection stages.

You've learned to nurture the soil. Now, it's time to expand the garden to ensure sufficient space for growth. In the next chapter, we'll explore the Dignity Ecosystem: the spacious conditions and interdependence that allow students (and teachers) to stretch, expand, and strengthen the culture that supports their growth.

Make some space for the next chapter. You're about to discover how partnering with students can help you grow, too.

CHAPTER 7

Dignity Ecosystem (Room For Growth)

*When you plant lettuce, if it does not grow well, you don't blame the lettuce.
You look for reasons it is not doing well. It may need fertilizer, or more water,
or less sun. You never blame the lettuce.*

—Thích Nhất Hạnh, 1992

Summer and Her Students Build Solutions Together

Summer sat at her desk as the morning sun filtered through the windows. The usual hum of second graders filled the room, but today a sense of anticipation also hung in the air. Today was different. Today, she was flipping the script. After months of guiding her students in self-reflection, collective reflection, and goal setting, today was her turn to be in the spotlight.

Earlier, she had handed out the Code of Collaboration rubrics, the tool they co-created to define their shared values of recognition, acceptance, inclusion, and acknowledgment. This time, instead of assessing themselves or each other, her students assessed her.

Summer watched as they studied the rubric, brows furrowed, pencils tapping. They took this seriously, which both comforted and unsettled her. How would they evaluate her? How well had she been upholding their Dignity Promise?

They completed their task quietly. When Summer collected the final paper, she slid the stack into her briefcase and moved on with the day. Later that evening, she curled up on her couch and began reading them. She started to feel uneasy.

The results were overwhelmingly positive: straight fours across the board, the highest marks possible. The more she read, the more uneasy she felt.[54] Were they being sincere? Had she unintentionally created an environment where they didn't feel safe enough to give authentic feedback?

The following day, the class gathered in a circle and Summer lifted the stack of rubrics and said, "Thank you all for your feedback. But I want to tell you something important. No one is perfect, not even teachers. I can't grow unless I get honest feedback. I need your help."

The students exchanged nervous glances. A few nodded hesitantly.

"Let's try this again," she said, smiling. "I promise you won't hurt my feelings. I won't get angry. Think about times I may have missed the mark. Your honesty helps me be a better teacher."

This time, the process felt different. Students were more thoughtful, their eyes lingering on specific rubric sections. They took longer to finish up. Later that evening, Summer saw a new pattern emerge—no more straight four stars. Several students had rated her lower on acknowledgment.

Curious, the next morning she arranged small group discussions to dig

---

54. Much like when you get a "K" text from a loved one. You just know something's off.

deeper. When it came time to report, one student hesitated before speaking. "Sometimes, when we come in the morning, you're on your computer. It kind of feels like...like you don't see us."[55]

A few students nodded. "Yeah, we feel a little invisible," one said.

Summer inhaled, not out of defensiveness but realization. They were right. She met their eyes. "Thank you for telling me that. If my actions make you feel unseen, that's not okay. We all made a Dignity Promise, including me. Let's make this better together."

She walked to the board. "First thing every morning, I have to take attendance and lunch count. That part can't change. But what can we do to ensure everyone feels seen as soon as they walk in?"

Ethan raised his hand first, enthusiasm lighting up his face. "What if we say good morning to each other when we walk in? Like, I say it to someone, and they say it back."

Summer's eyes brightened. "I love that, Ethan! I'll write that down."

Mia hesitated, but Summer gave her an encouraging nod. "Maybe we could have a morning question on the board. We could all write answers while you're working."

"That's a fantastic idea, Mia! That way, I can connect with you even while finishing my tasks."

Jayden raised his hand. "What if we had a check-in station? Like, we pick

---

55. In her defense, emails do magically turn a 5-minute task into a 45-minute time warp.

a card or write how we're feeling, and you could look at it later."[56]

Summer beamed. "I love that one, too, Jayden. A check-in station would help me learn how you're feeling immediately."

After brainstorming a few more ideas, Summer and her students voted on three solutions:

1. **A Good Morning Exchange:** Students greet each other upon arrival.
2. **A Morning Message Board:** A daily question to which everyone writes responses.
3. **A Check-in Station:** A space to share how students are feeling.

"This is what it means to live out our Dignity Promise," Summer told her students. "We saw something that wasn't working and built a solution together. I can't wait to see how this works tomorrow!"

Jayden grinned at Mia and said, "This is pretty cool. We're really a part of something in Ms. Snyder's class." Summer smiled, knowing they had just done something more than fix a problem. They had brought their Dignity Ecosystem into greater balance and strengthened their connection to the classroom community.

The Dignity Ecosystem: Fostering Growth through Feedback

Summer's experience illustrates how the Dignity Ecosystem operates in real-time, when feedback, trust, and shared accountability create the

---

56. Somewhere out there, a dusty Magic 8-Ball is wondering why it wasn't consulted.

conditions for meaningful growth.

Just as a garden flourishes when all its elements interact in an ecosystem, a culture of dignity has balanced interaction, too. A plant struggles if it has sunlight but no water. If the soil lacks oxygen, roots suffocate. Similarly, when dignity resources are misaligned and unbalanced, students experience gaps between expectations and reality, likely undermining their sense of belonging, engagement, and performance.

In Summer's case, her classroom had a strong Dignity Promise (shared vision) and consistent Dignity Connectors (structures to maintain relationships). However, student feedback revealed a gap between Dignity Expectations (behavioral success criteria) and Dignity Actions (practices and policies). The class addressed that gap to restore balance.

The balanced ecosystem reflects the interdependence of these resources, which sustains the fertile environment for student belonging to grow. Student belonging is more than feeling socially included: it also involves feeling valued, cared for, and recognized as an active participant in the school community. This broader conceptualization of belonging is known as school connectedness (Centers for Disease Control and Prevention [CDC], 2022).

Unlike positive social connectedness, which emphasizes peer interactions, school connectedness captures the full scope of students' relationships with their school, including their engagement with learning. Research consistently shows that, when students feel a deep connection to their school environment, they are more engaged, motivated, and likely to thrive academically and socially (CDC, 2009; Libbey, 2004).

How the Dignity Resources Work Together

Teachers strengthen the conditions enabling school connectedness to flourish by cultivating a balanced Dignity Ecosystem. Here is a description of how the essential resources interact to sustain a culture of dignity and a climate of belonging.

- **Dignity Promise** (Sunlight) provides values and vision, guiding the Dignity Expectations to make the values actionable.

  - Sunlight fuels plant growth but only when paired with air. Without carbon dioxide, even strong sunlight is ineffective for plant growth.
  - In Summer's class, students expected acknowledgment as part of the Dignity Promise, but the morning routine did not reflect that expectation.

- **Dignity Connectors** (Water) carry the nutrients of Dignity Actions to sustain relationships, fostering trust and psychological safety.

  - Water dissolves and transports nutrients. Without it, even nutrient-rich soil can't support growth.
  - Because Summer had built trust, students felt safe enough to provide honest feedback, revealing areas for improvement.

- **Dignity Expectations** (Air) clarify behaviors and reinforce the Dignity Promise.

  - Air oxygenates soil. In partnership with water, it enables roots to absorb nutrients. Without it, nutrients remain inaccessible, stunting plant growth.
  - Student feedback aerated the culture in Summer's classroom: The rubric exposed gaps between an intention (acknowledging students) and students' lived experiences (feeling unseen in the mornings).

- **Dignity Actions** (Soil) anchor and nourish growth, ensuring dignity is honored through Connectors, aligning with Expectations, and upholding the Promise.

  - Soil anchors plants and provides nutrients, but the soil must stay hydrated, aerated, and enriched to sustain growth toward the sun.
  - Summer's classroom had an established morning routine, but feedback revealed that acknowledgment, an essential nutrient, lacked potency during the routine.

- **Dignity Ecosystem** (Room for Growth) prevents competition for essential resources like affirmation, competence, and power, ensuring that dignity remains abundant and does not become distorted into something perceived as conditional, which is false or fake dignity and does damage.

  - When plants are too crowded, they compete (both above and below ground) for space and nutrients, harming each other and thwarting overall growth.
  - Without a process that builds on constructive feedback, Summer may never have recognized and addressed the dignity gap of acknowledgment in her classroom.

When these five elements work together, dignity naturally and organically becomes embedded in the classroom culture, ensuring sustained growth and continuous improvement.

Summer as a Dignity Gardener

Summer's example illustrates how each resource within the Dignity Ecosystem fuels the improvement process:

1. **Dignity Promise (Sunlight)** provided a vision for dignity

and belonging.

2. **Dignity Connectors (Water)** fostered trust and psychological safety.
3. **Dignity Expectations (Air)** clarified whether the vision was being met.
4. **Dignity Actions (Soil)** were adjusted using feedback and reflection.
5. **Dignity Ecosystem (Room for Growth)** ensured that reflection and co-creation were embedded within the classroom culture.

True improvement happens when these elements work together. If Summer had not ensured there was room for growth, her students might never have voiced their authentic feelings and experiences. They wouldn't have felt safe enough. It was the synergy of these elements that propelled her class forward.

However, openness to feedback alone doesn't guarantee improvement. Progress also requires intentional action. Summer acknowledged her students' experiences and displayed accountability by co-creating solutions with them. This strengthened classroom connectedness, as evidenced by Jayden's comment: "We're really a part of something."

Summer used solution building to transform feedback into meaningful action. It was a proactive process focused on creating more of what is wanted, which, for our purposes, is dignity-honoring actions. Instead of imposing change from above, the classroom community made change together. Although Summer worked with younger students, this process applies to any age group. Here's an example of solution building in a high school setting.

Case Study: Hats Off to This Solution-Building Example

The Dignity Ecosystem isn't just for classrooms: it also can transform entire schools. In 2018, we (John and Floyd) partnered with Principal Nathan Hostetler and his leadership team at Francis Howell North High School, just outside St. Louis, Missouri, to develop dignity-centered practices at a schoolwide level.

Throughout the year, Nathan and his team worked to cultivate a shared vision of dignity. They shifted their school culture into a culture of collaboration when dealing with issues that may have resulted in conflict and alienation in the past. One striking example was when Nathan facilitated a solution-building process around the school's no-hats policy.

During a workshop facilitated by our colleague Trent Day Hall, a small group of students questioned the fairness of the policy, raising valid concerns:

- Students undergoing cancer treatment and observing religious traditions were allowed to wear head coverings, but this exemption often singled them out, making them feel hyper-visible, isolated, and othered.

- But students with temporary head-covering needs (due to multi-day hair stylings, hair loss, personal insecurities, or simply having a bad hair day) had no such accommodation. For them, head-coverings, hats, and so on, were forbidden.

Nathan listened and took their concerns seriously. He tasked them with researching how other schools addressed similar policies. These students diligently undertook the research. Then, equipped with real-world examples of fairness and inclusivity, they made a thoughtful presentation to the faculty and staff.

Initially, most teachers strongly opposed changing the rule. But the students' well-reasoned arguments shifted their perspectives.[57] A staff vote

---

57. Persuasion level: Expert. These kids could have talked Ferris Bueller out of his day off.

revealed overwhelming support, and the school ultimately allowed hats.

This solution-building process did much more than change a rule: it also enabled student self-empowerment and developed students as stewards of their school culture. It also modeled genuine partnership between students, staff, and administration, demonstrating how dignity-centered leadership fosters sustainable, constructive change.

These students did more than win the right to wear hats. The impact extended beyond the school walls. They experienced dignity-centered leadership firsthand and carried this into their homes, workplaces, and communities. The process gave them the efficacy (confidence and skills) to co-create solutions wherever they went.

Identifying What's Missing: The First Step in Solution Building

The hat policy at Francis Howell High School and the morning routine in Summer's classroom weren't inflicting explicit harm. They became issues because they failed to align with the community's shared vision of dignity.

Both environments had already cultivated a dignity commitment, which is key to their eventual success. The presence of a shared vision allowed problem identification to go beyond simply addressing harm. It made it possible to recognize when something essential was missing and to take accountability to improve things.

- The Francis Howell North students saw the no-hats rule as mis-aligned with the school's values of fairness and inclusivity. Hatless heads weren't dangerous; the issue wasn't explicit harm but subtle disparity. Some students were made more visible in ways they didn't want. Without a schoolwide commitment to dignity, this gap would likely have gone unnoticed and unaddressed.

- In Summer's classroom, the issue wasn't explicit mistreatment. The absence of consistent acknowledgment contradicted the class's

Dignity Promise. Without a shared vision, students might not have recognized this as a gap, nor would Summer have invited them to co-create a solution.

These examples illustrate a vital shift that takes place within a culture of dignity:

- Ø Identifying problems involves recognizing what's implicitly missing to realize dignity more thoroughly; it's not just about eliminating explicit harm.
- Ø Proactive creation through solution building enables improvement efforts.

Improvement Efforts: From Problem Fixing to Solution Building

Traditional problem-fixing approaches usually focus on things unwanted: harm, dysfunction, noncompliance, adverse outcomes, and so on. These approaches often rely on punitive or compliance-based "solutions" to eliminate threats and remove obstacles. While this may stop immediate problems (or their symptoms), it doesn't necessarily create better conditions. Nor does it actively sustain dignity. Solution building offers an alternative. It puts dignity at the center of the improvement process (Table 7.1).

TABLE 7.1

Two Ways of Thinking About Improvement

Problem-Fixing Logic (Deficit-Based Thinking)	Solution-Building Logic (Dignity-Centered Thinking)
Is concerned with the presence of what is unwanted (problems)	Is concerned with the lack or absence of what is wanted (solutions)

Diagnoses and takes action to eliminate the problem	Identifies and scales what is wanted or already working
Relies on deficits, failures, threats, and compliance	Focuses on strengths, bright spots, growth, and possibility
Is often blame-oriented, reinforcing compliance over agency	Promotes shared responsibility and collective ownership
Has an idealistic goal of perfection	Has a pragmatic goal of progress

× Problem fixing asks, "What's wrong? How do we prevent or eliminate it?" This approach works backward, removing or correcting
what isn't working.

⊘ Solution building asks, "What's missing? What must we create to
realize a culture of dignity more fully?" This approach moves
forward, focusing on co-creation, aligning actions with values,
and ensuring the community actively upholds dignity.[58]

A Shift in Mindset: From Reaction to Co-Creation

The difference between problem fixing and solution building is subtle but
profound. In our examples, neither Summer's class nor Nathan's school
community required eliminating something explicitly harmful. Instead,
they required creating something better aligned with their shared visions
of dignity. That's the core of a solution-building approach:

- **It starts with a shared vision and moves forward,** ensuring that
  every step aligns with the community's values.

- **It reveals gaps,** identifying where dignity-centered solutions are
  needed—not to dwell on problems but instead to ensure clarity
  and purpose.

---

58. In short: Less *Ghostbusters* "Who you gonna call?" and more *MacGyver* "What can
we build with duct tape and a dream?"

- **It prioritizes collaboration and agency**, providing conditions for self-empowerment, where those most affected by the issue build the solution.

In our experience, many educators experience a moment of insight—a light-bulb moment—when they realize how solution building reinforces dignity (Figure 7.1). Unlike problem-fixing processes that focus on eliminating what's undesired, solution building actively constructs what's desired by

- reviewing and identifying opportunities for improvement,
- reflecting on how dignity-centered actions are lacking or missing, and
- revising behaviors, practices, and policies to better honor dignity.

FIGURE 7.1

Solution Building for Dignity

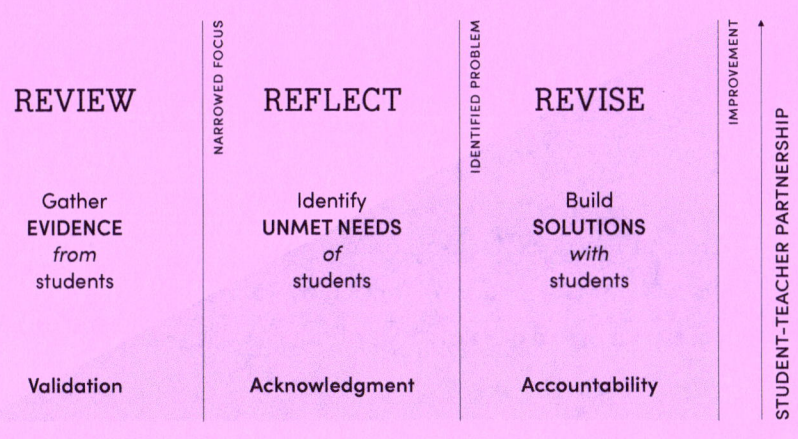

REVIEW	NARROWED FOCUS	REFLECT	IDENTIFIED PROBLEM	REVISE	IMPROVEMENT	STUDENT-TEACHER PARTNERSHIP
Gather **EVIDENCE** from students		Identify **UNMET NEEDS** of students		Build **SOLUTIONS** with students		
Validation		**Acknowledgment**		**Accountability**		

SOLUTION BUILDING FOR DIGNITY CLASSROOM ACTIVITY ⟶

You might be thinking, "Okay, but this is the real world, and I have real problems that need fixing now." Well, the same solution-building approach works in those situations, too, even when facing real and immediate threats, danger, or harm. To illustrate, let's examine a relatable challenge: hallway safety.

Case Study: Safer Hallways

You may be familiar with this situation. The school hallways feel like an Indy 500 race track: Students dash between classes, leading to collisions, frustration, and injuries. Books fly, tempers flare, and no matter how often teachers say, "No running!" students eventually run anyway.

The school leadership team meets to address the issue. They're feeling the weight of repeated disruptions and student safety concerns. The immediate goal? Stop the running.

At first glance, this seems like reasonable common sense. However, notice that "Stop the running" frames the endeavor as a quest to eliminate the bad thing, not to cultivate something better. This reactive, rule-based approach treats the symptom, not the cause. Sure, implementing or strengthening a no-running rule might curb the immediate issue, but does it build a culture of dignity in the long term? If anything, it might work against building a culture of dignity by enforcing compliance instead of promoting shared responsibility.

So, let's reframe the goal. Instead of merely preventing running, what if the goal were to create a culture of hallway safety? This subtle but powerful shift moves from restriction to intentionally fostering a safe, orderly, and student-owned environment.

- Instead of being anti-running, the focus is pro-safety.
- Instead of punishing students after the fact, the community co-creates an environment of accountability where safe behavior is the expected norm.

For this to happen, the school community must be able to imagine a better reality: imagination always precedes implementation (Brueg-gemann, 2018). In our hallway example, when the leadership team cultivates a shared vision of a safer, more-inclusive environment, they lay the groundwork for meaningful change. So, how can the leadership team start this process?

Instead of doubling down on rules, leadership can turn imagination into action by engaging students in co-creating solutions that make safety a shared responsibility. We call this process Collaborative Solution Building. It's a proactive approach where communities focus on their values and goals, scale bright spots, and move the current state closer to the desired state. Here's how it could unfold.

1. **Acknowledge the impact of the current situation.**
   First, validate the experiences of those harmed by the lack of hallway safety. This harm could include injuries, property damage, frustration, and unnecessary levels of stress and chaos. Ignoring these realities dismisses students' lived experiences and erodes trust in the school's ability to create a safe environment.

2. **Take responsibility for the conditions that led to the problem.**
   Instead of blaming students, reflect on whether a shared vision and clear expectations existed in the first place and, more importantly, whether students feel ownership over those expectations.[59] If they are unclear or not co-owned by students, acknowledge your role in the problem to earn and maintain student trust.

3. **Engage students in co-creating solutions.**
   Rather than imposing a new set of rules, invite students into the process:

---

59. Turns out, "Because I said so" has the same success rate in schools as it does at the dinner table when trying to convince a child that broccoli is fun.

- What would make the hallways feel safer?
- What might help everyone move through the school without chaos?
- What can we learn from times when the hallways function well?

Students may offer creative, practical solutions you haven't considered. Within our example, consider suggestions such as safety ambassadors, staggered dismissals, or hallway cues that use humor and encouragement rather than punitive measures.

4. **Implement and refine the plan.**

As new strategies roll out, gather student and staff feedback to adjust and improve. Keep the goal central. In our example, the goal wasn't just quiet, orderly hallways. That could have indicated a culture of control and compliance. The real goal was a culture where students take responsibility for maintaining a safe environment.

We could describe many more examples, but perhaps these are enough to convince you that Collaborative Solution Building works and is worth a try in your situation. Its strength is that it shifts improvement efforts (and continuous improvement is essential to building a culture of dignity) from negative reactions to positive co-creative responses. That honors dignity and makes it a powerful approach for addressing any school or classroom challenge.

Steps for Collaborative Solution Building

To apply Collaborative Solution Building in your classroom or situation, follow this six-step protocol:

1. **Identify the Gap:** Pinpoint precisely what's lacking or missing. What is needed to build a stronger culture of dignity?

   → Example: If students feel excluded during recess, focus on inclusion.

2. **Define the Goal:** Define a positive outcome aligned with the Dignity Promise.

→ Example: Ensure everyone feels welcome and valued in group activities.

3. **Find What Works:** Look for bright spots, moments when the issue didn't exist.
   → Ask: When do you feel most included? What's happening? Who's involved?

4. **Co-Create Solutions:** Work with students to generate practical strategies.
   → Example: Revise how recess groups form, assign roles, or create peer leaders.

5. **Implement and Adjust:** Take action, gather feedback, and refine strategies.
   → Example: Prototype an activity or group where everyone can join.

6. **Reflect and Celebrate:** Assess progress, refine strategies, and recognize growth.
   → Example: Celebrate progress to ensure that change feels meaningful and lasting.

By engaging students in this process, educators model dignity in action by the following actions:

- ☑ **Partnering with students** to co-create solutions
- ☑ **Displaying empathy** and listening deeply
- ☑ **Presuming competence**, valuing student insights and agency
- ☑ **Affirming students** and their abilities to engage in meaningful change
- ☑ **Repairing harm** and restoring lost trust by taking accountability

The beauty of Collaborative Solution Building is that it embeds dignity within the improvement process. It not only solves problems; the process itself fortifies the positive culture of classrooms and schools.[60]

Sustaining a Culture of Dignity

When teaching with dignity, the positive influence can ripple outward. Research shows that individual teachers have the power to create meaningful, schoolwide change (Muijs & Harris, 2006). When educators model dignity-centered practices, such as fostering relational trust, co-creating solutions with students, and prioritizing inclusive decision-making, these behaviors can spread through peer influence and student interactions, contributing to the development of a school culture that values dignity (Bryk & Schneider, 2002).

But what if you're the only teacher in your school currently implementing teaching with dignity principles? While grassroots efforts hold great potential, research suggests that the most sustainable and transformative impact occurs when leadership (e.g., principals and superintendents) models and prioritizes dignity (Figure 7.2). By using the authority conferred on them through their positions, leaders can embed dignity throughout the school or district's systems and structures, ensuring it becomes a defining characteristic of the school culture (Fullan, 2011a; Leithwood & Jantzi, 2005).

When leaders consistently set the expectation for dignity through policy and daily interactions, they establish an environment where dignity is the norm, making it easier for teachers to integrate dignity-centered practices into their classrooms. Research on school leadership by Leithwood and Jantzi (2006) suggests that, when administrators lead with dignity, teachers are more likely to align their practices with this expectation, strengthening relational trust and enhancing student engagement throughout the school community.

---

60. Like the perfect mixtape, once dignity makes its way in, its impact is hard to forget.

FIGURE 7.2

Sustaining an Organizational Culture of Dignity

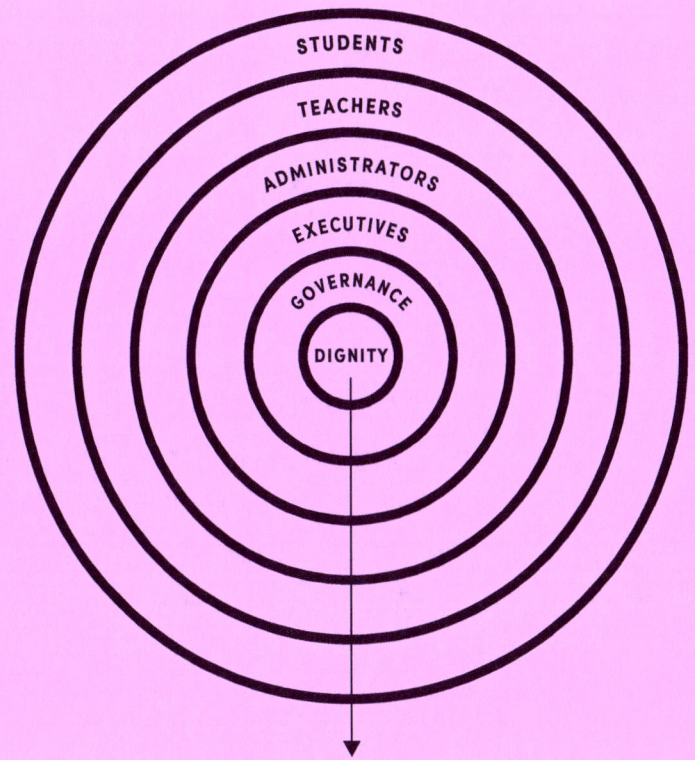

Furthermore, an influential education researcher, Michael Fullan, emphasizes that large-scale, lasting change in education is most effective when leaders embody the values they seek to cultivate (Fullan, 2011a).

Terroir: The Unique Character of an Ecosystem

As illustrated in Summer's elementary classroom and Nathan's hatless high school, the interplay of values, relationships, and leadership shapes a culture of dignity.[61] People who grow and develop within that environment carry its influence, which is evident in how they interact beyond the classroom. This concept parallels the concept of terroir in gardening.

- In agriculture, terroir (a term from the French) refers to the interaction between soil, climate, and geography that influence the character of a crop.
- For example, grapes grown in one region develop a distinct flavor profile that is nearly impossible to exactly replicate elsewhere.
- Terroir is more than ingredients; it also reflects the essence of a place, shaped by natural and human influences.

Similarly, in education the following are true:

- Each classroom and school has its own terroir, a culture shaped by relationships, shared values, and collective commitments.[62]
- When dignity is consistently honored, students become deeply rooted in a healthy culture that sustains belonging, trust, and shared responsibility.
- Dignity spreads organically, just as healthy soil enriches the entire ecosystem.

———

61. Dr. Jeff Naslund approached Summer and John after a 2024 workshop to share how the *Teaching with Dignity* gardening metaphor reminded him of terroir—a term and metaphor that influenced his leadership. He even considered putting "terroir" on t-shirts as part of a school-wide theme but reconsidered after realizing it looked too much like the word "terror." He figured he'd rather be seen as a principal, not mistaken for the Cryptkeeper, Freddy Krueger, or Jason. So, the concept remained motivation behind the scenes—in his school's soil.

62. Because of where and when we grew up, we still try to rewind movies after watching, out of habit; reactively imagine ColecoVision when we hear "big tech;" and secretly hope the San Diego Chicken gets its long-overdue ESPY. You can take the authors out of the 1980s, but...we're still amazed by autoreversing cassette decks.

Terroir in education reminds us of the following:

- ⌀ Culture is unique and transferable. Each classroom develops its own identity, but dignity-centered actions can spread outward, influencing others.
- ⌀ Dignity creates a shared ethos, sending a ripple effect beyond the classroom walls and into the broader community.

This natural expansion of dignity is what makes it both powerful and sustainable.

The Dignity Gardener's Gift: A World Transformed

Back in Colorado, something remarkable was happening in Summer Snyder's school. Other teachers and staff members noticed and admired Summer's students. Their classroom culture of dignity was rippling outwards.

"I can always tell when they're one of yours," a colleague said with a smile. "They speak so thoughtfully about dignity. And they treat others with so much kindness and respect. It's inspiring."

Summer's students noticed it, too.

Small acts of acknowledgment and inclusion were spreading to other classrooms.[63] Teachers began seeking advice on how to integrate dignity into their classrooms.

Then, one day, Summer received an unexpected invitation.

---

63. It's like *The Breakfast Club*, but without the existential monologues and the 1980s angst that made us who we are. Just dignity spreading like a perfectly executed slow clap.

The school counselor approached her, "Would your class be interested in partnering with the fifth graders? They'd love to learn from your second graders about dignity and how they uphold it. I think they'd benefit from seeing dignity in action."

Summer could hardly believe her ears. Anticipation and a deep sense of fulfillment washed over her. Of course, she thought, it made perfect sense that dignity culture couldn't be contained. She gathered her students and shared the news. They cheered, and a few pumped their fists in the air. They were eager to extend their learning beyond their classroom.

That moment of cheering crystallized a profound insight for Summer: Teaching with dignity served something bigger than Summer Snyder, her students, and their classroom. The dignity culture they had cultivated would grow far beyond these four walls. That was the nature of dignity. It wasn't confined to one person, moment, or space. Hurt can spread as quickly as blight, but dignity can spread even faster.[64]

She saw a bigger picture unfolding as she watched her students, faces alight with purpose, accept their mission to be ambassadors to the fifth graders. What they had been nurturing was bearing fruit; the growth was unstoppable, and seeds were spreading beyond the classroom. They were sprouting everywhere.

- In other classrooms.
- In the cafeteria and hallways.
- In the wider school community.

---

64. Blight: A plant disease that spreads rapidly and damages everything in its path. Think of it as the botanical equivalent of *Gremlins* eating after midnight. One moment, everything's fine; the next, chaos. That's how unchecked negativity can spread too. The good news is that positivity can spread just as fast.

She knew the influence wouldn't stop. Like seeds carried by unseen currents of wind, dignity doesn't stay confined to the garden where it was first planted. Some would take root nearby, while others would drift far beyond what Summer could see, blooming in places she would never visit. Summer sighed. What she could see, where she could go, now or in the future—none of that mattered. This dignity dream was so much bigger and more expansive than she'd ever imagined.

Although she would never experience the full legacy of what she'd planted and cultivated, she felt more committed than ever to doing her part: planting the seeds, nurturing the seedlings, promoting growth, and trusting her students to go forth and plant their own dignity gardens.

Summer smiled, ready for the next season of growth.

Appendix A

Context	Approach
United States	Rooted in the legacy of segregation and the civil rights movement, the U.S. education system is shaped by legal mandates to protect individual rights and promote access. Compliance with laws such as the 14th Amendment's Equal Protection Clause and federal anti-discrimination statutes underpins efforts to address racial, linguistic, and ability-based disparities in schooling.
Argentina	Shaped by a history of political upheaval and democratic restoration, Argentina treats education as both a public good and a constitutional right. The National Education Law (Ley de Educación Nacional) supports free public schooling, intercultural bilingual education for Indigenous communities, and democratic citizenship—framed in response to past authoritarianism and ongoing efforts to build a more inclusive society.
Canada and Australia	Informed by ongoing legacies of settler colonialism, both countries frame education within a multicultural democratic ideal while advancing Indigenous reconciliation. Policies emphasize multilingual education, cultural inclusion, and land-based learning, alongside national commitments—such as Canada's Truth and Reconciliation Calls to Action and Australia's Closing the Gap—to address historical harms and support Indigenous self-determination.
Germany	Built on postwar commitments to democracy and historical reckoning, Germany's education system balances academic and vocational pathways (via the dual system) with civic development through Bildung—a tradition viewing education as the formation of character, critical thinking, and social responsibility. Curricula include a focus on Holocaust education and democratic values.

Hawai'i and Alaska (U.S.)	Informed by Indigenous histories and ongoing movements for cultural revitalization, education in Hawai'i and Alaska includes place-based learning that centers Native values, languages, and worldviews. Frameworks such as Hawai'i's HĀ and Alaska's Cultural Standards for Educators promote student belonging, identity, and community responsibility through culturally grounded education shaped by local knowledge and priorities.
Independent Schools	Shaped by the interplay of market forces, cultural values, and parental priorities, independent schools uphold dignity through alignment with their mission and community. Accountability is maintained through accreditation, stakeholder engagement, and a focus on personalized learning or tradition, depending on context.
India	Rooted in constitutional commitments to social justice and universal access, India's education system promotes multilingual instruction, affirmative action for historically marginalized groups, and compulsory schooling through the Right to Education Act. Recent reforms aim to modernize curricula, expand vocational options, and reduce barriers linked to caste, gender, and geography.
International Schools	Situated at the intersection of global mobility and local context, international schools navigate linguistic and cultural complexity while upholding global accreditation standards. Dignity is supported through mission-driven values, responsiveness to diverse parent communities, and accountability to international frameworks.
Ireland	Influenced by its history of colonialism and independence, Ireland's system balances national identity with modern reforms. The curriculum promotes civic engagement, inclusion, and language preservation, while recent efforts focus on expanding access, supporting diverse learners, and addressing regional disparities.
Kenya	Framed by a post-independence vision of unity and development, Kenya's system emphasizes inclusive access and learner-centered reform. The Competency-Based Curriculum promotes practical skills, local knowledge, and holistic development, while addressing disparities tied to region, language, and socioeconomic status.

New Zealand	Grounded in bicultural commitments under the Treaty of Waitangi, New Zealand's education system integrates Māori perspectives and promotes holistic, culturally responsive learning. The early childhood curriculum *Te Whāriki* emphasizes relationships, identity, and belonging, while national policies support inclusion, language revitalization, and educational partnerships with Māori communities.
Nigeria	Guided by the Universal Basic Education policy and a constitutional commitment to education for all, Nigeria's system aspires to inclusive, tuition-free schooling through the junior secondary level. While implementation is uneven due to regional inequality, conflict, and infrastructure gaps, national policies emphasize local language instruction, civic education, and curriculum reform to promote unity, economic development, and social inclusion.
Nordic Countries: Denmark, Finland, Iceland, Norway, Sweden	Rooted in a tradition of social democracy and trust in public institutions, Nordic education systems prioritize high-quality public education as a universal right. Policies support fully funded schooling, minimal tracking, and minimal tuition through higher education, with a strong emphasis on inclusion, teacher professionalism, and civic responsibility.
Japan and South Korea	Evolving from postwar reconstruction and rapid industrial growth, both countries have long treated education as central to national economic success and social advancement. While academic achievement and standardized testing remain key features, recent reforms reflect efforts to address declining birthrates, growing immigrant populations, and student well-being—prompting greater attention to inclusive practices and holistic development.
South Africa	Shaped by the legacy of apartheid and a constitutional commitment to dignity and redress, South Africa's education system promotes multilingualism and inclusion. The national CAPS curriculum emphasizes historical awareness, critical thinking, and social justice, focusing on apartheid and building a democratic society.

| United Kingdom | Framed by a long history of class-based educational stratification, the U.K. system reflects tensions between tradition and inclusion. While public education is broadly accessible, regional variation (England, Scotland, Wales, Northern Ireland) shapes curriculum and governance. Recent efforts focus on closing attainment gaps, expanding vocational pathways, and addressing racial and socioeconomic disparities through targeted funding and reforms. |

Note: Portions of this appendix were drafted with the assistance of ChatGPT (OpenAI, 2024) and subsequently edited by the authors.

Appendix B

BARRIERS TO EFFECTIVE IMPLEMENTATION OF
EDUCATIONAL STRATEGIES

Barrier	Description	Examples from Research
Teacher-Level Challenges	Individual teacher limitations, including inadequate training, implicit bias, and resistance to change, can all hinder effective implementation.	Studies show that implicit bias toward ethnic minority students can negatively impact their academic experiences (Glock & Kleen, 2019; Sleeter & Grant, 2021).
Institutional Constraints	Schools often operate within rigid structures that limit innovation, including unsupportive leadership, high-stakes testing, and resource inequities.	High-stakes testing often forces teachers to focus on test preparation instead of deeper learning, limiting their ability to apply student-centered strategies (Milner, 2020; Nygreen & McLain, 2022).
Broader Societal Factors	Political resistance, standardized testing cultures, and policy roadblocks can create systemic barriers to meaningful educational reform.	Policy roadblocks and resistance to systemic change have been observed in the United States, United Kingdom, Australia, and parts of Europe, making it difficult to sustain reform efforts (Moses & Nanna, 2007).

Appendix C

Challenge to Education	Countries Affected (Ranked by Severity/Impact)
Decline in Academic Outcomes and Increased Disparities	South Africa, India, Brazil, United States, Australia, France, United Kingdom, Canada, New Zealand, Finland
Teacher Burnout and Shortages	United States, Australia, United Kingdom, South Africa, Canada, New Zealand, India, Brazil
Chronic Absenteeism and Student Disengagement	United States, Brazil, India, South Africa, United Kingdom, Australia
Mental Health Crises among Students	United States, United Kingdom, Australia, Canada, France, Finland, New Zealand, Japan, India
Disparities in Digital Access and Remote Learning	India, South Africa, Brazil, Australia, United States, Canada, United Kingdom
Dropout Rates and Educational Inequities	South Africa, India, Brazil, United States, Canada
Increased Child Labor due to Economic Hardship	India, Brazil, South Africa
Challenges in Adapting Traditional Education Models	Japan, Finland, United Kingdom, United States, Canada, Australia
Declining Trust between the Public and Schools	United States, United Kingdom, Canada, Australia, Brazil, New Zealand, South Africa, India

Sources: American Academy of Arts & Sciences, 2022; American Society for the Positive Care of Children, 2024; Betthäuser et al., 2023; GRC Global Group, 2022; Kuhfeld, et al., 2021; Poverty & Inequality Research Lab, 2023; U.S. Congress, 2023; United Nations Educational, Scientific and Cultural Organization, 2020.

Appendix D

Limit	Example	Lacks
Reactive	A stop-the-hate initiative may focus on stopping harm but lacks strategies to foster inclusivity and empathy.	Proactive Vision
Centers Opposition	An anti-corruption campaign may call for accountability but not propose viable, concrete governance reforms.	Positive Models
Negative Framing	An anti-bullying campaign that shows bullying behaviors might instead teach, model, and reinforce bullying behaviors and make it feel intractable or more pervasive than it is.	Positive Framing
Centers the Problem	An anti-racism effort may create or intensify an us vs. them dynamic, facilitating resistance, a psychological backlash, or even a strengthened opposing viewpoint.	Inclusive Framing
Problem Fixation	The war on drugs criminalized drug use while neglecting root causes such as addiction, poverty, or lack of access to health care.	Solution Orientation
Global Problem	Initiatives focused on large-scale, global problems such as anti-climate change can overwhelm people and lead to exhaustion, fatigue, and a feeling of hopelessness.	Specific Problem
Narrow Thinking	An anti-violence campaign may focus on stopping specific acts of violence while neglecting systemic factors (e.g., poverty or the lack of education) that contribute to violence.	Systemic Thinking
Dependency on External Forces	An anti-hate speech law may focus on holding others accountable through enforcement rather than through accountability and responsibility for positive cultural change.	Agency and Responsibility

Appendix E

Framework	Description	Empirical Support	Citation
Montessori Method	Child-centered learning with hands-on activities and mixed-age classrooms; fosters agency and choice	Engagement, executive function, collaboration, critical thinking, and problem solving	Montessori, 1912
Jena Plan	Mixed-age learning, personal responsibility, and community involvement	Positive student engagement and social development	Petersen, 1927
Reggio Emilia Approach	Inquiry-based, creative learning grounded in student interests	Boosts creativity, problem solving, and collaboration skills	Edwards et al., 1993
Constructivism	Knowledge built through experience, interaction, and reflection	Enhances critical thinking and problem-solving skills	Vygotsky, 1978
Cooperative Learning	Structured group work promoting interdependence and collaboration	Increases academic achievement and interpersonal relationships	Johnson & Johnson, 1975
Multicultural Education	Curricula inclusive of diverse cultural perspectives	Promotes democratic outcomes, cultural and civic awareness, and prejudice reduction	Banks, 1981

Cultural Competence Framework	Educational practices grounded in cultural awareness and responsiveness	Strengthens student-teacher relationships and academic outcomes	Cross et al., 1989
Funds of Knowledge	Learning connected to students' home and community knowledge	Increases student engagement and academic success	Moll et al., 1992
Culturally Relevant Pedagogy	Teaching that reflects and empowers students' cultural backgrounds	Boosts academic engagement, performance, and cultural identity	Ladson-Billings, 1995
Te Whāriki	Holistic, culturally responsive early childhood curriculum from New Zealand	Benefits for social and cognitive development	Ministry of Education New Zealand, 1996
Differentiated Instruction	Instruction adapted to students' readiness, interests, and learning profiles	Supports diverse learners and improves achievement	Tomlinson, 1999
Project-Based Learning	Real-world projects as the basis for deep learning and collaboration	Improves critical thinking, collaboration, and retention	Thomas, 2000
Culturally Responsive Teaching	Teaching practices aligned with students' cultural identities and experiences	Improves student engagement and achievement	Gay, 2000
Universal Design for Learning	Flexible learning environments responsive to learner variability	Enhances accessibility and learning outcomes	Rose & Meyer, 2002
Inquiry-Based Learning	Learning driven by questioning, investigation, and exploration	Enhances problem solving and critical thinking	Kuhn, 2005

Restorative Justice in Education	Practices that build community and repair harm within schools	Reduces disciplinary issues and fosters a positive school climate	Evans & Vaander-ing, 2012
Culturally Sustaining Pedagogy	Teaching that affirms and sustains students' cultural identities	Supports student identity and academic success	Paris, 2012
Competency-Based Education	Learning organized around demonstrated mastery rather than seat time	Leads to enhanced motivation and learning success	Sturgis, 2017
Trauma-Informed Pedagogy	Practices that respond to trauma's effects on learning and behavior	Improves learning environments and outcomes	Hays, 2019
Social-Emo-tional Learning	Instruction that devel-ops emotional regula-tion, relationships, and decision-making	Improves academic performance and mental well-being	CASEL, 2020

References

Allen, J. P., Porter, M. R., McFarland, F. C., McElhaney, K. B., & Marsh, P. (2008). The two faces of adolescents' success with peers: Adolescent popularity, social adaptation, and deviant behavior. *Child Development*, 76(3), 747–760. https://doi.org/10.1111/j.1467-8624.2005.00875.x

Alter, P., & Haydon, T. (2017). Characteristics of effective classroom rules: A review of the literature. *Teacher Education and Special Education*, 40(2), 114–127.

American Academy of Arts & Sciences. (2022). The global quest for educational equity: Policies and practices to improve access and inclusion. *Dædalus*, 151(2), 5–12. https://www.amacad.org/daedalus/introduction-global-quest-for-educational-equity

American Psychological Association (APA). (2023). *School connectedness: Supporting safe and supportive schools*. https://www.apa.org/pi/lgbt/programs/safe-supportive/school-connectedness

American Society for the Positive Care of Children (ASPCC). (2024). *The right to education: Laws that promote and protect access to education*. https://americanspcc.org/the-right-to-education-laws-that-promote-and-protect-access-to-education

Arnsten, A. F. T. (2009). Stress signaling pathways that impair prefrontal cortex structure and function. *Nature Reviews Neuroscience*, 10(6), 410–422. https://doi.org/10.1038/nrn2648

Aronson, E., Blaney, N., Stephan, C., Sikes, J., & Snapp, M. (1978). *The Jigsaw classroom*. Sage Publishing.

Austin, S. C. (2022). *National patterns of vulnerable decision points in school discipline* (Doctoral dissertation, University of Oregon). Scholars' Bank. https://scholarsbank.uoregon.edu/items/d4b6fd9e-618d-482a-8a2d-588e1beb63e1

Banks, J. A. (1981). Multicultural education: A conceptual framework. *Educational Researcher*, 10(6), 5–10.

Barkley, E. F., Cross, K. P., & Major, C. H. (2005). *Collaborative learning techniques: A handbook for college faculty* (1st ed.). Jossey-Bass.

Betthäuser, B. A., Bach-Mortensen, A. M., & Engzell, P. (2023). A systematic review and meta-analysis of the evidence on learning during the COVID-19 pandemic. *Nature Human Behaviour*, 7, 375–385. https://doi.org/10.1038/s41562-022-01506-4

Blum, R. W., McNeely, C. A., & Rinehart, P. M. (2002). Improving the odds: The untapped power of schools to improve the health of teens. Center for Adolescent Health and Development, University of Minnesota.

Bower, M. (1966). *The will to manage: Corporate success through programmed management*. McGraw-Hill.

Brueggemann, W. (2018). *The prophetic imagination* (40th anniversary ed.). Fortress Press.

Bryk, A. S., Gomez, L. M., Grunow, A., & LeMahieu, P. G. (2015). *Learning to improve: How America's schools can get better at getting better*. Harvard Education Press.

Bryk, A. S., & Schneider, B. (2002). *Trust in schools: A core resource for improvement*. Russell Sage Foundation.

Bryk, A. S., Sebring, P. B., Allensworth, E., Luppescu, S., & Easton, J. Q. (2010). *Organizing schools for improvement: Lessons from Chicago*. University of Chicago Press.

Buchs, C., Gilles, I., Antonietti, J.-P., & Butera, F. (2023). Effects of the Jigsaw Method on student educational outcomes: A systematic review and meta-analysis. *Frontiers in Psychology, 14*, 10436097. https://doi.org/10.3389/fpsyg.2023.1216437

Bullough, R. V., Jr. (2005). Teacher vulnerability and teachability: A case study of a mentor and two interns. *Teacher Education Quarterly, 32*(1), 23–39.

Burke, T. (n.d.). *Empathy is more powerful than sympathy. It allows us to connect, to set boundaries, and to be clear about what we need.* [Attributed quote; original source unverified].

Cacioppo, J. T., Cacioppo, S., & Gollan, J. K. (2014). The negativity bias: Conceptualization, quantification, and individual differences. *Behavioral and Brain Sciences, 37*(3), 309–310. https://doi.org/10.1017/S0140525X13002537

Cai, Y., Yang, Y., Ge, Q., & Weng, H. (2023). The interplay between teacher empathy, students' sense of school belonging, and learning achievement. *European Journal of Psychology of Education, 38*(3), 1167–1183. https://doi.org/10.1007/s10212-022-00637-6

Center for Applied Special Technology (CAST). (2018). *Universal design for learning guidelines version 2.2*. http://udlguidelines.cast.org

Centers for Disease Control and Prevention (CDC). (2009). *School connectedness: Strategies for increasing protective factors among youth*. https://stacks.cdc.gov/view/cdc/5767

Centers for Disease Control and Prevention (CDC). (2022). *School connectedness helps students thrive*. Centers for Disease Control and Prevention. https://safesupportivelearning.ed.gov/resources/school-connectedness-helps-students-thrive

Cobb, F., & Krownapple, J. (2019). *Belonging through a culture of dignity: The keys to successful equity implementation*. Mimi & Todd Press.

Cochran-Smith, M., & Lytle, S. L. (2009). *Inquiry as stance: Practitioner research for the next generation*. Teachers College Press.

Cohen, E. G. (1994). *Designing group work: Strategies for the heterogeneous classroom* (2nd ed.). Teachers College Press.

Collaborative for Academic, Social, and Emotional Learning (CASEL). (2020) *SEL 3 signature practices playbook: A toolkit for educators*. https://signaturepractices.casel.org/

Constitution of the State of Illinois. (1970). *Article I: Bill of Rights*. https://www.ilga.gov/commission/lrb/con1.htm

Cook, C. R., Duong, M. T., McIntosh, K., Fiat, A. E., Larson, M., Pullmann, M. D., & McGinnis, J. (2018). Addressing discipline disparities for Black male students: Linking malleable root causes to feasible and effective practices. *School Psychology Review, 47*(2), 135–152. https://doi.org/10.17105/SPR-2017-0026.V47-2

Cook, C. R., Fiat, A., Larson, M., Daikos, C., Slemrod, T., Holland, E. A., Thayer, A. J., & Renshaw, T. (2018). Positive greetings at the door: Evaluation of a low-cost, high-yield proactive classroom management strategy. *Journal of Positive Behavior Interventions, 20*(3), 149–159.

Cook-Sather, A. (2006). Sound, presence, and power: "Student voice" in educational research and reform. *Curriculum Inquiry, 36*(4), 359–390.

Cornelius-White, J. (2007). Learner-centered teacher-student relationships are effective: A meta-analysis. *Review of Educational Research, 77*(1), 113–143. https://doi.org/10.3102/003465430298563

Covey, S. R. (1989). *The 7 habits of highly effective people: Powerful lessons in personal change*. Free Press.

Cross, T. L., Bazron, B. J., Dennis, K. W., & Isaacs, M. R. (1989). *Towards a culturally competent system of care, Volume I*. Georgetown University Child Development Center.

Dalai Lama. (1999). *Ancient wisdom, modern world: Ethics for the new millennium*. Little, Brown, and Company.

Darling-Hammond, L., Ancess, J., & Ort, S. W. (2002). *High schools for equity: Policy supports for student learning in communities of color*. Stanford University, School Redesign Network. https://learningpolicyinstitute.org/media/4276/download?-file=High_Schools_for_Equity_SCOPE_REPORT.pdf

Deci, E. L., & Ryan, R. M. (2000). The "what" and "why" of goal pursuits: Human needs and the self-determination of behavior. *Psychological Inquiry, 11*(4), 227–268.

Demir, İ., Şener, E., Karaboğa, H. A., & Başal, A. (2023). Expectations of students from classroom rules: A scenario based Bayesian network analysis. *Participatory Educational Research, 10*(1), 1–20. https://doi.org/10.17275/per.23.23.10.1

Destin, M., & Oyserman, D. (2010). Incentivizing education: Seeing schoolwork as an investment, not a chore. *Journal of Experimental Social Psychology, 46*(5), 846–849.

Dobbin, F., & Kalev, A. (2016). Why diversity programs fail. *Harvard Business Review, 94*(7), 52–60. https://hbr.org/2016/07/why-diversity-programs-fail

Duguid, M. M., & Thomas-Hunt, M. C. (2015). Condoning stereotyping? How awareness of stereotyping prevalence impacts expression of stereotypes. *Journal of Applied Psychology, 100*(2), 343–359.

Dweck, C. S. (2006). *Mindset: The new psychology of success*. Random House.

Edelman, M. W. (1992). *The measure of our success: A letter to my children and yours*. Beacon Press.

Edutopia. (2019, January 14). *Making connections with greetings at the door* [Video]. https://www.edutopia.org/video/making-connections-greetings-door/

Edwards, C., Gandini, L., & Forman, G. (Eds.). (1993). *The hundred languages of children: The Reggio Emilia approach to early childhood education.* Ablex Publishing.

Edwards, C., Gandini, L., & Forman, G. (Eds.). (2012). *The hundred languages of children: The Reggio Emilia experience in transformation* (3rd ed.). Praeger.

European Union (EU). (2012). EU charter of fundamental rights (2012/C 326/02). *Official Journal of the European Union.* https://fra.europa.eu/en/eu-charter/article/1-human-dignity

Evans, K., & Vaandering, D. (2012). *The little book of restorative justice in education: Fostering responsibility, healing, and hope in schools.* Good Books.

Forscher, P. S., Mitamura, C., Dix, E. L., Cox, W. T. L., & Devine, P. G. (2016). Breaking the prejudice habit: Mechanisms, timecourse, and longevity. *Journal of Experimental Social Psychology, 63,* 141–154. https://doi.org/10.1016/j.jesp.2017.04.009

Frank, A. (1995). *The diary of a young girl: The definitive edition* (S. Massotty, Trans.). Doubleday. (Original work published 1947).

Freeman, S., Eddy, S. L., McDonough, M., Smith, M. K., Okoroafor, N., Jordt, H., & Wenderoth, M. P. (2014). Active learning increases student performance in science, engineering, and mathematics. *Proceedings of the National Academy of Sciences, 111*(23), 8410–8415. https://doi.org/10.1073/pnas.1319030111

Fullan, M. (2011a). *Change leader: Learning to do what matters most.* Jossey-Bass.

Fullan, M. (2011b). *The moral imperative realized.* Corwin Press.

Garrett, J. L. (1982). *The effects of participation in rule making on the compliance behavior of elementary students* (Publication No. 8301783) [Doctoral dissertation, University of Oregon]. ProQuest Dissertations & Theses Global. https://www.proquest.com/openview/295332256728b8383dd772f146ab188d

Gay, G. (2000). *Culturally responsive teaching: Theory, research, and practice.* Teachers College Press.

Gion, C., McIntosh, K., & Bastable, E. (2021). Effects of a multifaceted classroom intervention on racial disproportionality in school discipline. *Journal of Positive Behavior Interventions, 23*(3), 173–184.

Glock, S., & Kleen, H. (2019). Attitudes toward students from ethnic minority groups: The roles of preservice teachers' own ethnic backgrounds and teacher efficacy activation. *Studies in Educational Evaluation, 60,* 14–25.

Gopalan, M., & Brady, S. T. (2019). College students' sense of belonging: A national perspective. *Educational Researcher, 48*(6), 351–362. https://doi.org/10.3102/0013189X19897622

Gottman, J. M., & Levenson, R. W. (2002). A two-factor model for predicting when a couple will divorce: Exploratory analyses using 14-year longitudinal data. *Family Process, 41*(1), 83–96.

Grant, A. (2021). *Think again: The power of knowing what you don't know.* Viking.

Gray, D. L., Hope, E. C., & Matthews, J. S. (2018). Black and belonging at school: A case for interpersonal, instructional, and institutional opportunity structures. *Educational Psychologist, 53*(2), 97–113. https://doi.org/10.1080/00461520.2017.1421466

GRC Global Group. (2022). *Equity in education in the post-COVID era*. https://insights. grcglobalgroup.com/equity-in-education-in-the-post-covid-era/

Gregory, A., & Weinstein, R. S. (2008). The discipline gap and African Americans: Defiance or cooperation in the high school classroom. *Journal of School Psychology, 46*(4), 455–475.

Gruenert, S., & Whitaker, T. (2015). *School culture rewired: How to define, assess, and transform it*. Association for Supervision and Curriculum Development.

Harper, D. (n.d.). *Culture*. Online etymology dictionary. https://www.etymonline.com/ word/culture

Hattie, J. (2023). *Visible learning: The sequel: A synthesis of over 2,100 meta-analyses relating to achievement*. Routledge.

Hays, K. N. L. (2019). Trauma-informed pedagogy: The need for a culturally responsive approach in education. *Journal of Social Work in Education, 55*(3), 149–158.

Hicks, D. (2011). *Dignity: Its essential role in resolving conflict*. Yale University Press.

Hicks, D. (2018). *Leading with dignity: How to create a culture that brings out the best in people*. Yale University Press.

Hoyle, A. M., & O'Connor, M. C. (2018). Constructing moral agency in classroom communities: How teachers and students use rules to build democratic participation. *Journal of Pragmatics, 127*, 14–29. https://doi.org/10.1016/j.pragma.2018.01.012

Ingersoll, R. M., Merrill, L., & Stuckey, D. (2014). *Seven trends: The transformation of the teaching force* (CPRE Report #RR-80). Consortium for Policy Research in Education. https://www.cpre.org/sites/default/files/workingpapers/1506_7trend-sapril2014.pdf

Ito, T. A., Larsen, J. T., Smith, N. K., & Cacioppo, J. T. (1998). Negative information weighs more heavily on the brain: The negativity bias in evaluative categorizations. *Journal of Personality and Social Psychology, 75*(4), 887–900.

Johnson, D. W., & Johnson, R. T. (1975). *Learning together and alone: Cooperative, competitive, and individualistic learning*. Prentice-Hall.

Johnson, D. W., Johnson, R. T., & Holubec, E. J. (1994). *Cooperation in the classroom* (6th ed.). Interaction Book Company.

Kagan, S., & Kagan, L. (2009). *Kagan cooperative learning*. Kagan Publishing.

Kahneman, D., & Tversky, A. (1984). Choices, values, and frames. *American Psychologist, 39*(4), 341–350.

Kalev, A., Dobbin, F., & Kelly, E. (2006). Best practices or best guesses? Assessing the efficacy of corporate affirmative action and diversity policies. *American Sociological Review, 71*(4), 589–617.

Kaufman, J. H., Diliberti, M. K., Thompson, L. E., & Auerbach, J. (2024). American teacher well-being and intentions to leave in 2024. RAND Corporation. https://www. rand.org/pubs/research_reports/RRA1108-12.html

Keinan, G., Friedland, N., & Even-Haim, T. (2000). The effect of stress and self-esteem on social stereotyping. *Journal of Social and Clinical Psychology, 19*(2), 206–219. https://doi.org/10.1521/jscp.2000.19.2.206

Kershner, I. (Director). (1980). *Star Wars: Episode V—The empire strikes back* [Film]. Lucasfilm; 20th Century Fox.

Kilanowski, J. F. (2012). Breaking the ice: A pre-intervention strategy to engage research participants. *Journal of Pediatric Health Care, 26*(3), 209–212. https://doi.org/10.1016/j.pedhc.2012.01.001

King, M. L., Jr. (1963). *Strength to love.* Harper & Row.

Kohn, A. (1996). *Beyond discipline: From Compliance to Community.* Association for Supervision and Curriculum Development.

Kuhn, D. (2005). *Education for thinking.* Harvard University Press.

Ladson-Billings, G. (1995). Toward a theory of culturally relevant pedagogy. *American Educational Research Journal, 32*(3), 465–491.

Legault, L., Gutsell, J. N., & Inzlicht, M. (2011). Ironic effects of antiprejudice messages: How motivational interventions can reduce (but also increase) prejudice. *Psychological Science, 22*(12), 1472–1477.

Leithwood, K., & Jantzi, D. (2005). A review of transformational school leadership research 1996–2005. Paper presented at the annual meeting of the American Educational Research Association, Montreal, Canada.

Leithwood, K. & Jantzi, D. (2006) Transformational school leadership for large-scale reform: Effects on students, teachers, and their classroom practices. *School Effectiveness and School Improvement, 17*(2), 201–227. https://doi.org/10.1080/09243450600565829

Leverson, M., Smith, K., McIntosh, K., Rose, J., & Pinkelman, S. (2021). *PBIS cultural responsiveness field guide: Resources for trainers and coaches.* University of Oregon.

Libbey, H. P. (2004). Measuring student relationships to school: Attachment, bonding, connectedness, and engagement. *Journal of School Health, 74*(7), 274–283.

LiCalsi, C., Osher, D., & Bailey, P. (2021, August). *An empirical examination of the effects of suspension and suspension severity on behavioral and academic outcomes.* American Institutes for Research. https://www.air.org/sites/default/files/2021-08/NYC-Suspension-Effects-Behavioral-Academic-Outcomes-August-2021.pdf

Lukianoff, G., & Haidt, J. (2018). *The coddling of the American mind: How good intentions and bad ideas are setting up a generation for failure.* Penguin Press.

Ma, Y., Siu, A. M. H., & Shek, D. T. L. (2022). Social connectedness, social support, and positive youth development: A study of Chinese adolescents. *Frontiers in Psychology, 13*, 1029315. https://doi.org/10.3389/fpsyg.2022.1029315

Mahar, M. T. (2011). Impact of short bouts of physical activity on attention-to-task in elementary school children. *Preventive Medicine, 52*, S60–S64. https://doi.org/10.1016/j.ypmed.2011.01.026

Maroney, D. (2019). *The imagine project: Empowering kids to rise above drama, trauma, and stress.* Imagine Project, Inc.

Marquand, R. (Director). (1983). *Star Wars: Episode VI—Return of the Jedi* [Film]. Lucasfilm; 20th Century Fox.

McDonald, J. P., Mohr, N., Dichter, A., & McDonald, E. C. (2013). *The power of protocols: An educator's guide to better practice* (3rd ed.). Teachers College Press.

McIntosh, K. (2019). *Neutralizing routines: Strategies to interrupt snap-judgement responses for staff and students.* California PBIS Conference.

McIntosh, K., Girvan, E. J., Horner, R. H., & Smolkowski, K. (2014). Education not incarceration: A conceptual model for reducing racial and ethnic disproportionality in school discipline. *Journal of Applied Research on Children: Informing Policy for Children at Risk, 5*(2), Article 4.

McIntosh, K., Girvan, E. J., McDaniel, S. C., Santiago-Rosario, M. R., St. Joseph, S. D., Fairbanks Falcon, S., Izzard, S., & Bastable, E. (2021). Effects of an equity-focused PBIS approach to school improvement on exclusionary discipline and school climate. *Preventing School Failure: Alternative Education for Children and Youth, 65*(4), 354–361.

Michigan Department of Education. (2021). *Accelerated learning vs. remediation.* Michigan Department of Education. https://www.michigan.gov/mde/-/media/Project/Websites/mde/Flexible-Learning-Options/Accelerated-Learning/AL-vs-Remediation/AL_v_Remediation.pdf

Milner, H. R. (2020). *Start where you are, but don't stay there: Understanding diversity, opportunity gaps, and teaching in today's classrooms* (2nd ed.). Harvard Education Press.

Ministry of Education, New Zealand. (1996). *Te Whāriki: He whāriki mātauranga mō ngā mokopuna o Aotearoa: Early childhood curriculum.* Learning Media.

MIT Teaching & Learning Lab. (n.d.). *Students' sense of belonging matters: Evidence from three studies.* https://tll.mit.edu/sense-of-belonging-matters

Moll, L. C., Amanti, C., Neff, D., & Gonzalez, N. (1992). *Funds of knowledge for teaching: Using a qualitative approach to connect homes and classrooms. Theory into Practice, 31*(2), 132–141.

Montazeri Khadem, A., Khoshkholgh, R., Vafisani, F., & Dolatabadi, Z. (2022). Using the Jigsaw (puzzle) method in academic environments: A review of studies on the effectiveness of the Jigsaw educational method on university students. *Medical Education Bulletin, 3*(2), 465–472. https://www.medicaleducation-bulletin.ir/article_146209.html

Montessori, M. (1912). *The Montessori method* (A. E. George, Trans.). Frederick A. Stokes Company. (Original work published 1909)

Moses, M. S., & Nanna, M. J. (2007). The testing culture and the persistence of high stakes testing reforms. *Education and Culture, 23*(1), 55–72.

Muijs, D., & Harris, A. (2006). Teacher led school improvement: Teacher leadership in the UK. *Teaching and Teacher Education, 22*(8), 961–972. https://doi.org/10.1016/j.tate.2006.04.010

Muldrew, A. C., & Miller, F. G. (2020). Self-monitoring. In K. C. Radley & E. S. Dart (Eds.), *School-based behavioral intervention case studies: Implementation and practice* (pp. 161–177). Routledge. https://doi.org/10.4324/9780429291319-11

Muldrew, A. C., & Miller, F. G. (2021). Examining the effects of the personal matrix activity with diverse students. *Psychology in the Schools, 58*(3), 515–533.

National Center for Pyramid Innovations. (2023). *National Training Institute on Effective Practices: Addressing challenging behavior.* https://challengingbehavior.org/training/conference/

New York State Education Department. (2012). *The Dignity for All Students Act (DASA), Article 2, Section 10.* https://www.nysed.gov/student-support-services/dignity-all-students-act-dasa

Nhat Hanh, T. (1992). *Peace is every step: The path of mindfulness in everyday life.* Bantam Books.

Nygreen, K., & McLain, B. (2022). *Educational justice movements and the politics of transformation.* Routledge.

Olson, K. (2009). *Wounded by school: Recapturing the joy in learning and standing up to old school culture.* Teachers College Press.

OpenAI. (2024). *ChatGPT* (GPT-4) [Large language model]. https://chat.openai.com/chat

Organisation for Economic Co-operation and Development [OECD]. (2024). *Education Policy Outlook 2024: Teachers as Designers of Learning Environments.* OECD Publishing. https://www.oecd.org/publications/education-policy-outlook-2024-0411a0c4-en.htm

Owens, J. & McLanahan, S. (2020). Unpacking the drivers of racial disparities in school suspension and expulsion. *Social Forces, 98*(4), 1548–1577. https://doi.org/10.1093/sf/soz095

Paluk, E. L., Porat, R., Clark, C. S., & Green, D. P. (2021). Prejudice reduction: Progress and challenges. *Annual Review of Psychology, 72*, 533–560. https://doi.org/10.1146/annurev-psych-071620-030619

Paris, D. (2012). Culturally sustaining pedagogy: A needed change in stance, theory, and practice. *Educational Researcher, 41*(3), 93–97.

Petersen, P. (1927). *Der Kleine Jena-Plan.* Eugen Diederichs.

Poverty & Inequality Research Lab. (2023). *Educational inequities related to race and socioeconomic status deepened by COVID-19 pandemic.* University of California, Davis, Center for Poverty & Inequality Research. https://poverty.ucdavis.edu/post/educational-inequities-related-race-and-socioeconomic-status-deepened-covid-19-pandemic

Putwain, D. W., & von der Embse, N. P. (2018). Teachers' use of fear appeals and timing reminders prior to high-stakes examinations: Pressure from above, below, and within. *Social Psychology of Education, 21*(5), 1001–1019. https://doi.org/10.1007/s11218-018-9448-8

Remen, R. N. (2000). *My grandfather's blessings: Stories of strength, refuge, and belonging.* Riverhead Books.

Renshaw, T. L., Long, A. C. J., & Cook, C. R. (2015). Assessing teachers' positive psychological functioning at work: Development and validation of the Teacher Subjective Wellbeing Questionnaire. *School Psychology Quarterly, 30*(2), 289–306.

Rogers, C. R., & Farson, R. E. (1957). *Active listening.* Industrial Relations Center, University of Chicago.

Rose, D. H., & Meyer, A. (2002). *Teaching every student in the digital age: Universal design for learning*. Association for Supervision and Curriculum Development.

Ryan, R. M., & Deci, E. L. (2000). Self-determination theory and the facilitation of intrinsic motivation, social development, and well-being. *American Psychologist*, *55*(1), 68–78.

Santiago-Rosario, M. R., & McIntosh, K. (2021). *Increasing disciplinary equity by teaching neutralizing routines to teachers and students*. In *Motivating the SEL field forward through equity* (Vol. 21, pp. 127–142). Emerald Publishing Limited.

Senge, P. M. (1990). *The fifth discipline: The art and practice of the learning organization*. Doubleday.

Siegel, D. J., & Bryson, T. P. (2011). *The whole-brain child: 12 revolutionary strategies to nurture your child's developing mind*. Delacorte Press.

Sleeter, C. E., & Grant, C. A. (2021). *Making choices for multicultural education: Five approaches to race, class, and gender* (7th ed.). Wiley.

Smolkowski, K., Girvan, E. J., McIntosh, K., Nese, R. N. T., & Horner, R. H. (2016). Vulnerable decision points for disproportionate office discipline referrals: Comparisons of discipline for African American and White elementary school students. *Behavioral Disorders*, *41*(4), 178–195. https://doi.org/10.17988/bedi-41-04-178-195.1

Sparks, S. D. (2020, November 10). Training bias out of teachers: Research shows little promise so far. *Education Week*. https://www.edweek.org/leadership/training-bias-out-of-teachers-research-shows-little-promise-so-far/2020/11

Starr, K. (2022). Neoliberalism, education policy, and leadership observations. In F. W. English (Ed.), *The Palgrave handbook of educational leadership and management discourse* (pp. 1053–1071). Palgrave Macmillan. https://doi.org/10.1007/978-3-030-39666-4_98-1

Sturgis, C. (2017). *Quality principles for competency-based education*. iNACOL (International Association for K–12 Online Learning). https://aurora-institute.org/resource/quality-principles-for-competency-based-education/

Thomas, J. W. (2000). *A review of research on project-based learning*. The Autodesk Foundation.

Tomlinson, C. A. (1999). *The differentiated classroom: Responding to the needs of all learners*. Association for Supervision and Curriculum Development.

Tutu, D. (1984). *Hope and suffering: Sermons and speeches*. Skotaville.

U.S. Congress. (2023). *Transformational reforms and updates to ensure educational quality and urgent investments in Today's Youth Act of 2023*. H.R.1429, 118th Congress. https://www.congress.gov/bill/118th-congress/house-bill/1429

United Nations (UN). (1948). *Universal declaration of human rights*. https://www.un-.org/en/about-us/universal-declaration-of-human-rights

United Nations (UN). (1989). *Convention on the rights of the child*. https://www.ohchr.org/en/instruments-mechanisms/instruments/convention-rights-child

United Nations Educational, Scientific and Cultural Organization (UNESCO). (2020). *Impact of the COVID-19 pandemic on education worldwide*. https://unesdoc.unesco.org/ark:/48223/pf0000380398

Valencia, R. R. (1997). *The evolution of deficit thinking: Educational thought and prac-tice*. Routledge.

Vygotsky, L. S. (1978). *Mind in society: The development of higher psychological pro-cesses*. Harvard University Press.

Walton, G. (2021, November 9). Stop telling students, "You belong!" *Education Week*. https://www.edweek.org/leadership/opinion-stop-telling-students-you-be-long/2021/11

Walton, G. M., & Cohen, G. L. (2011). A brief social-belonging intervention improves ac-ademic and health outcomes of minority students. *Science, 331*(6023), 1447–1451. https://doi.org/10.1126/science.1198364

Zimmerman, B. J. (2002). Becoming a self-regulated learner: An overview. *Theory Into Practice, 41*(2), 64–70. https://doi.org/10.1207/s15430421tip4102_2

Index

www.ingramcontent.com/pod-product-compliance
Lightning Source LLC
Chambersburg PA
CBHW060144130626

46556CB00006B/2491